25 Bridge Conventions You Should Know

PRACTICE

MAKES

PERFECT

Master Point Press
214 Merton St. Suite 205
Toronto, Ontario, Canada
M4S 1A6   (647)956-4933

Email: info@masterpointpress.com
Websites: www.masterpointpress.com
                www.teachbridge.com
                www.bridgeblogging.com
                www.ebooksbridge.com

Library and Archives Canada Cataloguing in Publication

Seagram, Barbara, author
      25 bridge conventions you should know : practice makes perfect
/ Barbara Seagram and David Bird.

Issued in print and electronic formats.
ISBN 978-1-77140-029-9 (paperback).--ISBN 978-1-55494-628-0 (pdf).--
ISBN 978-1-55494-673-0 (html).--ISBN 978-1-77140-863-9 (html)

      1. Contract bridge--Bidding. I. Bird, David, 1946-, author II. Title.
III. Title: Twenty-five bridge conventions you should know.

GV1282.4.S422 2016   795.41'52   C2015-908498-9
                                                       C2015-908499-7

Canada█ | We acknowledge the financial support of the Government of Canada.
         | Nous reconnaissons l'appui financier du gouvernement du Canada.

Editor   Ray Lee
Copy editor/interior format   Sally Sparrow
Cover and interior design   Olena S. Sullivan/New Mediatrix

3 4 5 6   19 18 17
PRINTED IN CANADA

25 Bridge Conventions You Should Know

PRACTICE
MAKES
PERFECT

BARBARA SEAGRAM & DAVID BIRD

Master Point Press • Toronto, Canada

CONTENTS

Introduction   7

SECTION 1: LEARN THESE FIRST

1: Stayman 2♣ response to 1NT   11
2: Takeout Doubles   16
3: Weak Two-bids   22
4: Strong 2♣ opener   27
5: Reverses   32
6: Blackwood and Gerber   37
7: Negative Doubles   42
8: Jacoby and Texas Transfers   47

SECTION 2: MORE COMPLICATED

9: Jacoby 2NT — Forcing Major Raise   54
10: Splinter Bids   59
11: Cuebid Raises   64
12: Balancing   69
13: Help-suit Game Tries   74
14: Control-showing Cuebids   79
15: The Grand Slam Force   84
16: Michaels cuebids and Unusual NT   89
17: Landy 2♣ over Opponents' 1NT   94

SECTION 3: SOPHISTICATED STUFF

18: Lebensohl 2NT   101
19: Reverse Drury   106
20: Roman Keycard Blackwood   111
21: Fourth Suit Forcing   116
22: New Minor Forcing   121
23: Ogust Responses   126
24: Responsive Doubles   131
25: Lead-directing Doubles   136

INTRODUCTION

The book *25 Bridge Conventions You Should Know*, by Barbara Seagram and Marc Smith, is a classic that has sold more than 160,000 copies — the best-selling bridge book for many decades. This playbook is designed to accompany it.

Each of the twenty-five chapters begins with a summary of an important bidding convention. This is followed by four deals in which the convention is put to instructive use. There is then further analysis of the play or defense of the contract that is reached. A bridge teacher might use such deals after explaining a particular convention to her students. Alternatively, you will be able to try the various problems in the deals yourself, as you read this book. You may be asked, for example: 'Look at the West hand for a moment. What would you lead against 4♠?' Once you have made up your mind, the text may continue: 'Right, now take the South cards and see if you would have made the contract.'

Your overall aim here is the same as with most such books — to improve the standard of your game and to enjoy yourself at the same time. Good luck!

Barbara & David

LEARN THESE

1

FIRST

STAYMAN 2♣ RESPONSE TO 1NT

One of the world's most popular and useful conventions is the Stayman 2♣ opposite a 1NT opening from partner. It is used to seek a 4-4 fit in a major suit. After a start of 1NT – 2♣, the opener rebids:

2◊	I have no four-card major
2♡	I have four hearts (maybe four spades too)
2♠	I have four spades, but not four hearts

Sometimes the opener will hold a five-card major when he rebids 2♡ or 2♠.

You use Stayman when you hold one or more four-card majors yourself. If instead you held five cards in one of the majors, you would start with a transfer response (see Chapter 8).

The responder may take various actions after the opener's rebid. He may pass when his hand is weak and he is happy to play in spades, hearts or diamonds (his shape may be 4=3=5=1 or 4=4=5=0):

Partner	You
1NT	2♣
2◊	all pass

With 8-9 points, responder may invite a game at his second turn:

(a) Partner	You	(b) Partner	You
1NT	2♣	1NT	2♣
2♠	2NT	2♠	3♠

In (a) the responder bids 2♣ holding four hearts. When no 4-4 heart fit comes to light, he invites a game in notrump. In (b) a 4-4 spade fit has been found and the responder invites the opener to bid 4♠ with a non-minimum.

When the responder is stronger, with 10+ points, he may bid a game:

(a) Partner	You	(b) Partner	You
1NT	2♣	1NT	2♣
2♠	3NT	2♠	4♠

PLAY DEAL 1-1

Neither Vul. Dealer South.

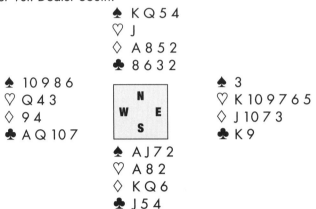

```
                    ♠ K Q 5 4
                    ♡ J
                    ◇ A 8 5 2
                    ♣ 8 6 3 2
    ♠ 10 9 8 6                         ♠ 3
    ♡ Q 4 3          N                 ♡ K 10 9 7 6 5
    ◇ 9 4         W     E              ◇ J 10 7 3
    ♣ A Q 10 7       S                 ♣ K 9
                    ♠ A J 7 2
                    ♡ A 8 2
                    ◇ K Q 6
                    ♣ J 5 4
```

West	North	East	South
			1NT
pass	2♣	pass	2♠
pass	4♠	all pass	

The Bidding: North uses a Stayman 2♣ to seek a 4-4 fit in spades. When South rebids 2♠ a spade fit is located and North bids game in the suit. If South had rebid 2◇ or 2♡ instead, North would have bid 3NT. (It is rarely right to look for an eleven-trick minor-suit game instead of 3NT, unless you have a very shapely hand.)

The Play: West leads the ♠10 and, as declarer, you must make a plan before playing to the first trick. You expect to lose three club tricks and should plan to ruff two hearts in the dummy. These ruffs should be taken with the ♠5 and ♠4, leaving the trump honors to draw the defenders' trumps. It is therefore vital to win the first trick in the dummy with the ♠Q (or the ♠K).

You cross to the ♡A and ruff a heart with the ♠4. You return to your hand with the ◇Q and ruff your last heart with the ♠5. You then play the dummy's remaining top trump and reenter your hand with the ◇K to draw West's remaining trumps with the ♠AJ.

You can then try your luck in the diamond suit. If it breaks 3-3, you will be able to discard a club and score an overtrick. When the cards lie as in the diagram, you cannot avoid the loss of three club tricks. You make the contract exactly.

PLAY DEAL 1-2

E-W Vul. Dealer South.

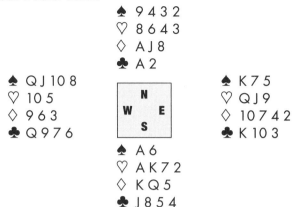

```
                    ♠ 9 4 3 2
                    ♡ 8 6 4 3
                    ◊ A J 8
                    ♣ A 2
   ♠ Q J 10 8                        ♠ K 7 5
   ♡ 10 5              N             ♡ Q J 9
   ◊ 9 6 3        W         E        ◊ 10 7 4 2
   ♣ Q 9 7 6          S             ♣ K 10 3
                    ♠ A 6
                    ♡ A K 7 2
                    ◊ K Q 5
                    ♣ J 8 5 4
```

West	North	East	South
			1NT
pass	2♣	pass	2♡
pass	3♡	pass	4♡
all pass			

The Bidding: North uses Stayman 2♣ to seek a 4-4 fit in hearts or spades. What should he say at his second turn, when a heart fit has been found? He is not quite strong enough to leap to 4♡ and should invite a game by raising to 3♡. South holds a maximum 17 HCP and is happy to bid the heart game.

The Play: West leads the ♠Q and, as declarer, the time has come to make a plan. You expect to lose a spade and a club and must therefore hope that trumps break 3-2 and you have only one loser in that suit. You start with five potential losers, looking at the South hand. To reduce this to the required three, you should aim to ruff two clubs in dummy.

Suppose you win the spade lead and play your two top trumps, finding a 3-2 break. You will go down! When you surrender a club trick, preparing to take the two ruffs that you need, East will win and draw a third round of trumps. With only one trump left in dummy, you can no longer take two ruffs.

After winning the spade lead, you should play ace and another club. When you regain the lead, you will play the ace and king of trumps and subsequently take two club ruffs in dummy. East can score his master trump when he wishes. The contract is yours!

PLAY DEAL 1-3

N-S Vul. Dealer South.

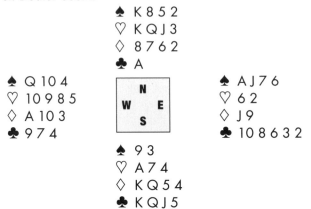

```
                    ♠ K 8 5 2
                    ♡ K Q J 3
                    ◊ 8 7 6 2
                    ♣ A
    ♠ Q 10 4           N           ♠ A J 7 6
    ♡ 10 9 8 5     W       E       ♡ 6 2
    ◊ A 10 3           S           ◊ J 9
    ♣ 9 7 4                        ♣ 10 8 6 3 2
                    ♠ 9 3
                    ♡ A 7 4
                    ◊ K Q 5 4
                    ♣ K Q J 5
```

West	North	East	South
			1NT
pass	2♣	pass	2◊
pass	3NT	all pass	

The Bidding: North uses a Stayman 2♣ to seek a 4-4 fit in either hearts or spades. When South rebids 2◊, denying a major, North rebids 3NT.

The Play: West leads the ♡10 and declarer counts eight top tricks in hearts and clubs. He wins the first trick with dummy's ♡J and plays the ♣A, so that he will be able to score the three club honors in his hand later. His next move is to lead a diamond to the king, setting up a ninth trick from that suit. The deal is not yet over! What should declarer do when West wins with the ◊A and switches to the ♠Q? (He can see that there is no future in hearts and declarer has played both diamonds and clubs.)

How easy it would be to cover with dummy's ♠K, but you would then go down. East would win with the ♠A and return the ♠6 to partner's ♠10 (swallowing your ♠9). The ♠4, through dummy's remaining ♠85 would then allow East to score two more spade tricks with his ♠J7.

How can you avoid losing four spade tricks? You should calculate what will happen if you do not cover the ♠Q. West will continue with the ♠10. Now it is right to play the ♠K, because East will have no entry back to the West hand. When he wins with the ♠A, he cannot play effectively from his remaining ♠J7. Dummy's ♠85 will be a stopper and you have nine tricks.

PLAY DEAL 1-4

Neither Vul. Dealer South.

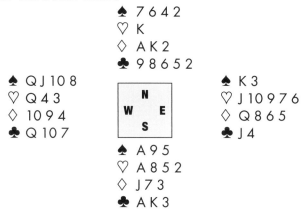

```
                  ♠ 7 6 4 2
                  ♡ K
                  ◇ A K 2
                  ♣ 9 8 6 5 2
  ♠ Q J 10 8                      ♠ K 3
  ♡ Q 4 3           N             ♡ J 10 9 7 6
  ◇ 10 9 4      W       E         ◇ Q 8 6 5
  ♣ Q 10 7          S             ♣ J 4
                  ♠ A 9 5
                  ♡ A 8 5 2
                  ◇ J 7 3
                  ♣ A K 3
```

West	North	East	South
			1NT
pass	2♣	pass	2♡
pass	3NT	all pass	

The Bidding: North uses a Stayman 2♣ to seek a 4-4 fit in spades. When South responds 2♡ to show a heart suit, North rebids 3NT. If South held four spades as well as four hearts, he would then bid 4♠. He would know that North would not have bid Stayman unless he held at least one four-card major.

The Play: West leads the ♠Q and East plays the ♠K so that it will not block the suit on the second round. You are not afraid of any switch and hold up your ♠A on the first round, winning the spade continuation. What next?

You have seven top tricks and can establish two more tricks in clubs, provided the suit splits 3-2. Should you continue with the ♣A, the ♣K and a low club? No, because you would then have no entry to reach the ♡A in your hand. West would win with the ♣Q, score two spade winners and exit safely in diamonds, putting the contract one down.

To make the contract you should lead the ♣3 on the first round of clubs, setting up two extra winners in the suit. West will win, score two more spade tricks and return a heart. You win with the ♡K, cross to the ♣A and play the ♡A. You then play the ♣K and return to dummy with a diamond to score two more club tricks. You make four clubs, one spade and two tricks in each red suit.

TAKEOUT DOUBLES

Nearly all doubles below game level are for takeout, asking partner to describe his hand. Here are some examples:

A.	You	LHO	Partner	RHO
			1◇	dbl

B.	You	LHO	Partner	RHO
		1♣	pass	1♡
	dbl			

C.	You	LHO	Partner	RHO
		1◇	pass	3◇
	dbl			

D.	You	LHO	Partner	RHO
			3♡	dbl

E.	You	LHO	Partner	RHO
		1♠	pass	pass
	dbl			

In A, partner doubles 1◇ for takeout. He is probably quite short in diamonds and wants you to choose a trump suit (or bid notrump), also to give some idea of your strength. In B, the opponents have bid two suits; your double asks partner to choose one of the other suits. RHO raises diamonds to the three-level in C. Your double is still for takeout. Partner will expect you to hold both major suits and will try to respond in one of those. In D, your LHO opens with a preemptive 3♡; partner has a good hand and doubles to ask you to make a bid; he will be hoping that you can respond in spades, the other major. Finally, in E your LHO's opening bid is followed by two passes. Your double in the fourth seat is again for takeout.

What type of hand is suitable for a takeout double? Normally your hand will satisfy these guidelines:

- a hand worth an opening bid
- adequate support for all unbid suits (particularly unbid majors)
- no more than two cards in the opponents' suit

When you respond to a takeout double, you have two duties. You must choose a trump suit (or notrump). You must also let partner know roughly how strong you are, so he can judge whether a game is possible.

Suppose your LHO opens 1♢ and your partner makes a takeout double. These are the main responses available to you:

0-8 points	bid your best suit (outside diamonds) at the minimum level
8-10	bid 1NT with stopper(s) in the opener's suit
9-11	jump in your best suit
11-12	bid 2NT with stopper(s) in the opener's suit
12+	force to game

♠ J 8 6 3   ♡ 9 7 2   ♢ 4 3 2   ♣ 7 6 2

Here you respond 1♠. It would be a horrible mistake to pass, just because you are weak. The contract of 1♢ doubled would be made, often with several overtricks!

♠ A Q 7 2   ♡ K 3   ♢ 10 4 3 2   ♣ 7 6 2

Now you bid 2♠ to let partner know you hold 9-11 points. This information may allow him to bid a game, or make a game try (perhaps by raising to 3♠).

♠ K Q 10 9 6   ♡ 9 5   ♢ J 4   ♣ A Q 9 5

This is much too strong for a non-forcing 2♠ response. You have enough for game and expect partner to hold adequate spade support. You leap to 4♠. What can you do when you have a strong hand but do not know which suit to make trumps? You bid the opener's suit. (It is always a strong move when you bid the opponents' suit during an auction. This is called a cuebid.)

♠ A J 7 3   ♡ K J 8 3   ♢ 9 7 6   ♣ A 8

You want to be in a game but have no wish to leap to 4♡ or 4♠ immediately, simply guessing which major suit to try. Instead you should bid 2♢, showing the strength of your hand. If partner rebids 2♡, you will raise to 4♡. If instead he rebids 2♠ (which he would do with four spades and only three hearts), you will raise to 4♠.

PLAY DEAL 2-1

Both Vul. Dealer West

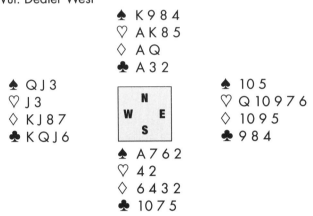

```
                    ♠ K 9 8 4
                    ♡ A K 8 5
                    ◇ A Q
                    ♣ A 3 2
  ♠ Q J 3                              ♠ 10 5
  ♡ J 3              N                 ♡ Q 10 9 7 6
  ◇ K J 8 7      W       E             ◇ 10 9 5
  ♣ K Q J 6          S                 ♣ 9 8 4
                    ♠ A 7 6 2
                    ♡ 4 2
                    ◇ 6 4 3 2
                    ♣ 10 7 5
```

West	North	East	South
1◇	dbl	pass	1♠
pass	3♠	pass	4♠
all pass			

The Bidding: North makes a takeout double and hears a 1♠ response. He has a good fit for spades and must judge how high to raise in that suit. It would be an overbid to jump to 4♠, because South might hold no points at all. (South was forced to make a response of some sort, however weak his hand). North's right rebid is 3♠. Now South must realize that his partner has a very strong hand. Holding a precious ace, and a ruffing value, he should raise to 4♠.

The Play: West leads the ♣K. How will you tackle the spade game? You win with dummy's ♣A and play the king and ace of trumps, the defenders' trumps splitting 3-2. Should you play a third round of trumps now?

No! West holds the ♠Q and there is no purpose in playing another round of trumps. You want to use the remaining trumps in both hands to score some ruffs. In any case, you want to take a diamond finesse. A diamond to the queen wins the next trick. You play the ◇A, followed by the ♡A and ♡K. You then ruff two hearts in your hand and two diamonds in dummy. West can take the ♠Q when he wishes. You will score five side-suit tricks, two top trumps, and four ruffs (one of which will be overruffed by West). That is a total of ten. Had you made the mistake of leading a third round of trumps to West's queen, you would have been able to take only two ruffs — one in each hand — and would have gone one down.

PLAY DEAL 2-2

N-S Vul. Dealer West

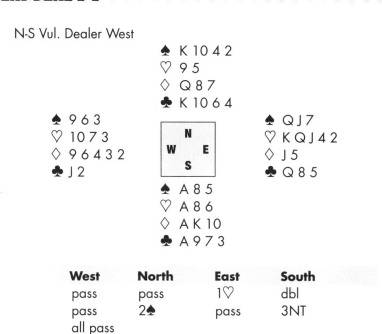

```
              ♠ K 10 4 2
              ♥ 9 5
              ◇ Q 8 7
              ♣ K 10 6 4
♠ 9 6 3                        ♠ Q J 7
♥ 10 7 3          N           ♥ K Q J 4 2
◇ 9 6 4 3 2    W     E        ◇ J 5
♣ J 2            S            ♣ Q 8 5
              ♠ A 8 5
              ♥ A 8 6
              ◇ A K 10
              ♣ A 9 7 3
```

West	North	East	South
pass	pass	1♥	dbl
pass	2♠	pass	3NT
all pass			

The Bidding: With 19 HCP South is too strong for a 1NT overcall. He starts with a takeout double, intending to rebid in notrump. With two tens in his hand, North is just worth a jump response of 2♠. South would have rebid 1NT over a 1♠ response, showing around 19 points. After North's response of 2♠, South knows that game values are present and jumps to 3NT.

The Play: West leads the ♥3 to East's ♥J. How would you play 3NT?

You have eight tricks on top and the club suit offers the best chance of establishing an extra trick. Since you will probably have to lose a trick in clubs, your first task is to break the link between the defenders in hearts. You hold up on the first round of hearts, also on the second round. (It is a good general rule to hold up twice if possible). You win the third round of hearts and must now establish the club suit. What's more, you must do so without allowing East (the danger hand, who can cash two more hearts) to win the lead. You cross to the ♣K and play a club to the ♣9. You are ducking a trick into the safe hand. West wins the trick and has no heart to play, thanks to your hold-up of the ♥A. You win his return and can then claim nine tricks for the contract.

PLAY DEAL 2-3

Neither Vul. Dealer West

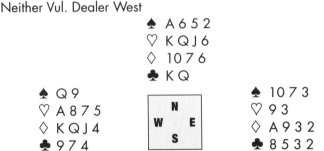

```
                    ♠ A 6 5 2
                    ♡ K Q J 6
                    ◇ 10 7 6
                    ♣ K Q
    ♠ Q 9                           ♠ 10 7 3
    ♡ A 8 7 5          N            ♡ 9 3
    ◇ K Q J 4      W       E        ◇ A 9 3 2
    ♣ 9 7 4            S            ♣ 8 5 3 2
                    ♠ K J 8 4
                    ♡ 10 4 2
                    ◇ 8 5
                    ♣ A J 10 6
```

West	North	East	South
1◇	dbl	pass	2♠
pass	4♠	all pass	

The Bidding: North makes a takeout double and South must calculate his re-sponse. He has four clubs as well as four spades but will respond in the major suit. There are two good reasons for this. When partner doubles he is very likely to have length in the unbid majors. Also, a major-suit fit is more likely to lead to a game contract. Should South respond 1♠? No, because this would show only 0-8 points and South has 9 points. He describes his hand well by responding 2♠ and North is happy to raise to game.

The Play: West leads the ◇K, East encouraging with the ◇9. West continues with the ◇Q, East playing the ◇3, and then a third diamond to East's ace. How will you play 4♠ from this point?

You ruff the third round of diamonds with the ♠4. You have lost two tricks already and will have to lose a heart trick. You must therefore play the trump suit without losing a trick. How will you attempt to do that?

When you are missing five cards including the queen, the usual play is to take a finesse in the suit. Is that the best play here? No! Only 16 points are held by the defenders and East has already shown the ◇A. Surely West holds the remaining 12 points to justify his opening bid. You play the ace and king of trumps and are rewarded by the fall of West's queen. You draw East's last trump with the jack and play hearts to set up that suit. The contract is yours.

PLAY DEAL 2-4

Neither Vul. Dealer East

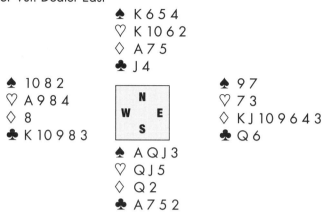

♠ K 6 5 4
♡ K 10 6 2
◊ A 7 5
♣ J 4

♠ 10 8 2
♡ A 9 8 4
◊ 8
♣ K 10 9 8 3

♠ 9 7
♡ 7 3
◊ K J 10 9 6 4 3
♣ Q 6

♠ A Q J 3
♡ Q J 5
◊ Q 2
♣ A 7 5 2

West	North	East	South
		3◊	dbl
pass	4◊	pass	4♠
all pass			

The Bidding: East opens with a preemptive 3◊ and South doubles for takeout. What should North respond? He is strong enough to insist on a game contract but does not know which major suit will make the better trump suit. There is no need to guess! North bids 4◊, telling partner that he is strong and looking for a trump fit, with the focus on the majors. South would bid 4♡ now if he held both majors. As it is, he bids 4♠ and this ends the auction.

The Play: How would you play 4♠ when West leads the ◊8?

If you play low from dummy, East will win with the ◊K and give West a diamond ruff. Subsequent losers in hearts and clubs will then put the game one down. The bidding tells you that East is likely to hold seven diamonds, so you should win the first trick with the ◊A. You then draw trumps in three rounds and play hearts. Even if West has another diamond to play when he wins with the ♡A, you will make the game with four trump tricks, three hearts, two minor-suit aces and one club ruff in dummy.

WEAK TWO-BIDS

An opening bid of 2◊, 2♡ or 2♠ is a preempt. It is usually made on a hand that contains a good six-card suit but is worth less than an opening bid.

A sound weak two-bid contains 6-10 points and two of the three top trump honors (or three of the top five). Note that an opening bid of 2♣ is not available to show a weak hand with six clubs, since this is used to show strong opening hands (see Chapter 4). These are typical sound weak two-bids:

(1) ♠ 10 4	(2) ♠ 10 5	(3) ♠ A J 10 8 6 2
♡ 5 3	♡ K Q J 8 7 2	♡ J 7 6
◊ A K J 10 8 7	◊ 8	◊ 10 9 4
♣ J 10 4	♣ Q 9 5 4	♣ Q

You would open 2◊, 2♡ and 2♠ respectively. Partner may then pass, bid a new suit (forcing below the game-level), raise your suit to the three-level (preemptive, to be passed) or raise to game. On a hand where partner needs more information, he can respond 2NT (see Chapter 23).

Since one purpose of a weak two-bid is to be preemptive, some players are willing to reduce the requirements (suit quality and general strength) so they can use them more often. This is safer when you are not vulnerable and applies particularly in the third seat, when almost anything is acceptable. When you are weak and partner has passed, the opponents can probably make a game or slam. You must make their auction as difficult as possible.

When partner opens with a weak two-bid in a major, you may raise to game in two quite different situations: on strong hands where you hope game can be made, also on weaker hands with a good trump fit where you hope to make life awkward for the opponents. You would raise 2♠ to 4♠ on either of these hands:

(1) ♠ A 9 7 4	(2) ♠ Q 10 9 5
♡ 8 4	♡ 7
◊ A 7	◊ K J 10 7 6
♣ A K 9 8 2	♣ Q J 5

On (1) you expect 4♠ to be made. On (2) the opponents can do well in hearts. Good luck to them when you raise the preempt to 4♠!

PLAY DEAL 3-1

E-W Vul. Dealer South.

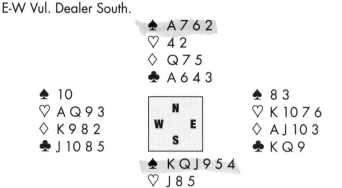

```
                    ♠ A 7 6 2
                    ♡ 4 2
                    ◇ Q 7 5
                    ♣ A 6 4 3
  ♠ 10                              ♠ 8 3
  ♡ A Q 9 3         N               ♡ K 10 7 6
  ◇ K 9 8 2    W         E          ◇ A J 10 3
  ♣ J 10 8 5        S               ♣ K Q 9
                    ♠ K Q J 9 5 4
                    ♡ J 8 5
                    ◇ 6 4
                    ♣ 7 2
```

West	North	East	South
			2♠
pass	4♠	all pass	

The Bidding: Does North expect ten tricks to be made in spades when his partner opens 2♠? No, but he nevertheless bids 4♠. Why is that? It's because he can see that the opponents will be able to make a good contract their way. He expects to score his two aces in defense but any further defensive tricks might be hard to come by. As it happens, his 4♠ raise shuts out the opponents and the contract is not even doubled.

The Play: West leads the ♣J and declarer wins with dummy's ♣A. There is nothing much to the play after that. Declarer draws trumps in two rounds and eventually ruffs a heart in dummy for his eighth trick. He goes two down for the loss of 100 when the opponents could have made at least 620, playing in hearts.

'Couldn't you have doubled 4♠?' West asked. 'Even if I pass the double, at least we'd score 300 instead of 100.'

It was a bit unreasonable to blame East for his pass. For all he knew, North might hold 17 points and be bidding the contract to make.

PLAY DEAL 3-2

Both Vul. Dealer North.

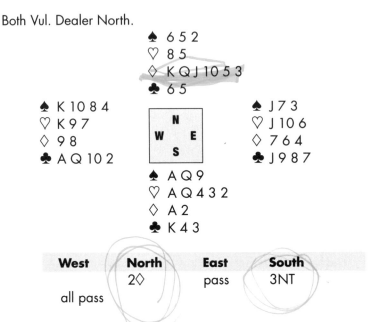

♠ 6 5 2
♡ 8 5
◇ K Q J 10 5 3
♣ 6 5

♠ K 10 8 4
♡ K 9 7
◇ 9 8
♣ A Q 10 2

N
W E
S

♠ J 7 3
♡ J 10 6
◇ 7 6 4
♣ J 9 8 7

♠ A Q 9
♡ A Q 4 3 2
◇ A 2
♣ K 4 3

West	North	East	South
	2◇	pass	3NT
all pass			

The Bidding: North has an absolutely fine hand for opening 2◇, even when vulnerable. Players who say 'I like a little more when vulnerable' merely make life easy for their opponents. Remember that the main point of preempting is to take away bidding space from the opponents. With 19 points and a fitting honor in diamonds, South has high hopes of making 3NT.

The Play: If West leads a spade, a heart or a club, he will hand you a ninth trick on a plate. How would you tackle 3NT if West chooses the safe lead of the ◇9?

You win with the ◇A and play dummy's diamonds, throwing three hearts and a club from your hand. To guarantee the contract after this start, you would then play low to the ♠9. When West won with the ♠10, he would have to give you a trick by leading a major-suit card into one of your AQ tenaces or a club, allowing you to score the ♣K.

As you see, it would make no difference if East played the ♠J on the first round of spades. You would cover with the ♠Q and when West won with the ♠K he would again be endplayed. Your ♠A9 would act as a tenace in this case.

PLAY DEAL 3-3

Neither Vul. Dealer South.

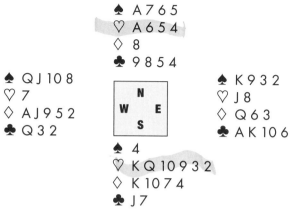

```
                    ♠ A 7 6 5
                    ♡ A 6 5 4
                    ◇ 8
                    ♣ 9 8 5 4
   ♠ Q J 10 8                      ♠ K 9 3 2
   ♡ 7              ┌─────┐        ♡ J 8
   ◇ A J 9 5 2      │  N  │        ◇ Q 6 3
   ♣ Q 3 2         W│     │E       ♣ A K 10 6
                    │  S  │
                    └─────┘
                    ♠ 4
                    ♡ K Q 10 9 3 2
                    ◇ K 10 7 4
                    ♣ J 7
```

West	North	East	South
			2♡
pass	4♡	all pass	

The Bidding: North has two reasons to raise to 4♡ with his excellent heart support. Once in a while, his partner may make the heart game. Just as important, though, is the fact that East-West may well have a good contract available their way. (On this layout, they can make 4♠.) Neither West nor East has quite enough to contest the auction and 4♡ becomes the final contract.

The Play: How will you play 4♡ when West leads the ♠Q?

You win with dummy's ♠A. Should you draw trumps now? No, because if West holds the ◇A, you may need to ruff three diamonds in the dummy. Even if you draw just one round of trumps at the start, the defenders will have a chance to draw a second round when you lose the first round of diamonds.

You should lead a diamond to the king at Trick 2. West wins with the ◇A and plays a second round of spades. You ruff in your hand and ruff a diamond in dummy. You then return to your hand with another spade ruff and ruff a third round of diamonds low in the dummy. A trump to the king reveals that the defenders' trumps break 2-1. You ruff your last diamond with dummy's ♡A (ruffing high to avoid a possible overruff). You can then draw the last trump and claim the contract. You make one side-suit trick with the ♠A and no fewer than nine trump tricks.

PLAY DEAL 3-4

E-W Vul. Dealer North.

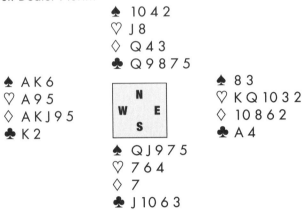

```
                  ♠ 10 4 2
                  ♡ J 8
                  ◇ Q 4 3
                  ♣ Q 9 8 7 5

  ♠ A K 6              N          ♠ 8 3
  ♡ A 9 5                         ♡ K Q 10 3 2
  ◇ A K J 9 5    W         E      ◇ 10 8 6 2
  ♣ K 2              S            ♣ A 4

                  ♠ Q J 9 7 5
                  ♡ 7 6 4
                  ◇ 7
                  ♣ J 10 6 3
```

West	North	East	South
	pass	pass	2♠
3NT	all pass		

The Bidding: After two passes, South knows that East-West can make a game at least. He knows too that the vulnerability is in his favor. Is it wildly inventive and mischievous to open 2♠ in such a situation? No, it is normal bridge! West can hardly be blamed for bidding 3NT and, although East may have given some thought to bidding further, who can blame him for passing?

The Play: North leads the ♠2 against 3NT and West has a sinking feeling when he inspects the dummy. There is nothing much to the play. The 3-1 diamond break spares East-West the embarrassment of writing 3NT+4 on their card, but an excellent small slam has been missed. If South were to pass, West would open 2♣ and it would be the work of a few moments to reach 6NT, 6♡ or 6◇, all of which would be easily made.

What is the message of the deal? Non-vulnerable in the third seat, anything goes!

STRONG 2♣ OPENER

An opening bid of 2♣ shows a powerful hand, where you would be worried about a one-bid being passed out. It is artificial and says nothing about the club suit. This is the scheme of opening bids when you are balanced:

2NT	20-21 HCP
2♣ – 2◇ – 2NT	22-23 HCP
2♣ – 2◇ – 3NT	24-25 HCP
3NT	26-27 HCP
2♣ – 2◇ – 4NT	28-30 HCP

The bidding may stop in 2NT when responder has a bust. When you open 2♣ and rebid in a suit, this is game-forcing. These are typical 2♣ openers:

(1) ♠ A K Q 9 8 2
♡ A 6
◇ 8
♣ A Q J 4

(2) ♠ A Q 5
♡ K J 8 2
◇ A Q J 4
♣ A Q

(3) ♠ 8 7
♡ A K
◇ A K Q J 7 6
♣ A 6 2

On (1) you can almost make 4♠ on your own hand. You open 2♣, intending to rebid in spades. On (2) you intend to rebid 2NT. With hand (3) you hope that 3NT (at least) can be made. Your intended rebid is 3◇.

Unless partner has 8+ points and a good suit, he will respond 2◇. After 2♣ – 2◇ – 2♠, a raise to 3♠ shows some points. He might hold: ♠J64 ♡32 ◇AJ976 ♣975. With only: ♠654 ♡Q86 ◇95 ♣109862 he would rebid 4♠.

Here your partner is unbalanced with good cards:

Partner	Partner	You
♠ 8 6		2♣
♡ K J 7 3 2	2◇	2♠
◇ A 8 2	3♡	
♣ 6 5 4		

Partner would have rebid an artificial 3♣ (a second negative) with fewer than 4 HCP. Here he shows more than that with 5+ hearts.

PLAY DEAL 4-1

Neither Vul. Dealer South.

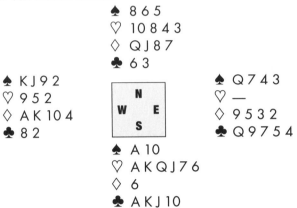

```
                    ♠ 8 6 5
                    ♡ 10 8 4 3
                    ◇ Q J 8 7
                    ♣ 6 3
  ♠ K J 9 2                        ♠ Q 7 4 3
  ♡ 9 5 2            N             ♡ —
  ◇ A K 10 4    W         E        ◇ 9 5 3 2
  ♣ 8 2             S             ♣ Q 9 7 5 4
                    ♠ A 10
                    ♡ A K Q J 7 6
                    ◇ 6
                    ♣ A K J 10
```

West	North	East	South
			2♣
pass	2◇	pass	2♡
pass	4♡	pass	6♡
all pass			

The Bidding: South's 2♡ rebid is forcing to game. North does not have enough to make the strong move of 3♡. He leaps to 4♡ and South decides to try his luck in 6♡. Blackwood would be pointless since he does not expect North to hold an ace for his weak jump to 4♡.

The Play: Against a contract at the five- or six-level, it is normal to lead the king from ace-king. Your partner will then signal how many cards he has in the suit — playing high with an even number, low with an odd number. West leads the ◇K, East playing the ◇5. When West switches to a trump, East discards a club. How can you avoid a spade loser?

You must discard two spades from dummy on your club suit. You will need to finesse in clubs and that may require two entries to the dummy. You win the first round of trumps with the ♡J, retaining the two lower trumps. You then lead the ♡6 to dummy's ♡8, finessing against West's known ♡9. A finesse of the ♣J wins and you return to dummy with the ♡10, drawing West's last trump. You repeat the club finesse and discard two spades from dummy on the ♣AK. A spade ruff with dummy's last trump will be your twelfth trick.

PLAY DEAL 4-2

E-W Vul. Dealer South.

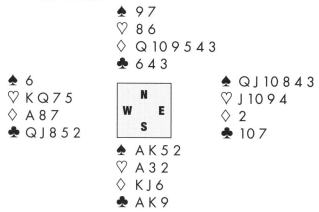

```
                    ♠ 9 7
                    ♡ 8 6
                    ◇ Q 10 9 5 4 3
                    ♣ 6 4 3
    ♠ 6                                ♠ Q J 10 8 4 3
    ♡ K Q 7 5        N                 ♡ J 10 9 4
    ◇ A 8 7      W       E             ◇ 2
    ♣ Q J 8 5 2      S                 ♣ 10 7
                    ♠ A K 5 2
                    ♡ A 3 2
                    ◇ K J 6
                    ♣ A K 9
```

West	North	East	South
			2♣
pass	2◇	pass	2NT
pass	3NT	all pass	

The Bidding: South's 2NT rebid, after opening 2♣, shows 22-23 HCP. Partner can pass with a bust. Here he decides to raise to 3NT, hoping that his hand will provide several diamond tricks. It's unlikely that eleven tricks will be available in diamonds, so 3NT is the most promising game.

The Play: Take the West cards now and see how you would have defended. If you're unusually virtuous, you can cover the East and South hands with your fingers, look away for a few moments to forget what you have seen in that respect and then return to defend on the West cards. (You may be the only reader of the book to do that...)

Right, you lead the ♣5 and partner plays the ♣10, declarer winning with the ace. What is your plan for the defense when declarer next leads the ◇K from his hand?

You should hold up the ◇A, aiming to prevent declarer from reaching dummy to score lots of diamond tricks. East follows with the ◇2 and declarer continues with the ◇6. What now? Since it is entirely possible that South started with ◇KJ6, you should hold up your ace again. Provided you defend in this manner, the contract will go down.

PLAY DEAL 4-3

N-S Vul. Dealer South

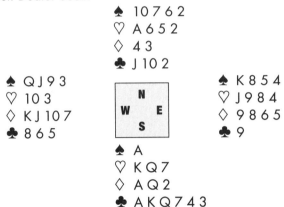

♠ 10 7 6 2
♡ A 6 5 2
◇ 4 3
♣ J 10 2

♠ Q J 9 3
♡ 10 3
◇ K J 10 7
♣ 8 6 5

♠ K 8 5 4
♡ J 9 8 4
◇ 9 8 6 5
♣ 9

♠ A
♡ K Q 7
◇ A Q 2
♣ A K Q 7 4 3

West	North	East	South
			2♣
pass	2◇	pass	3♣
pass	4♣	pass	4NT
pass	5◇	pass	6♣
all pass			

The Bidding: What should you bid on the North cards when partner opens 2♣ and rebids 3♣? South has shown a great hand! He has forced to game with a club suit. He might have had to play in 5♣ even if you held practically nothing. Any original thoughts that you had picked up a hopeless hand should be dismissed. You agree clubs as trumps by bidding 4♣. South then bids 4NT. We will see in Chapter 6 that this is Blackwood, asking you how many aces you hold. You duly show your one ace with a 5◇ response and partner then bids 6♣.

The Play: How will you play 6♣ when West leads the ♠Q to your ♠A? You cross to the ♣10 and finesse the ◇Q. If the finesse wins, you will make an overtrick. Here it loses and West plays another spade. You ruff and draw a second round of trumps with the ♣A, East showing out. You then play the ◇A and ruff the ◇2 with dummy's ♣J. You return to hand with a high spade ruff, draw West's last trump and claim the remaining tricks.

PLAY DEAL 4-4

Both Vul. Dealer South.

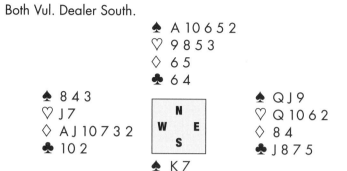

```
                    ♠ A 10 6 5 2
                    ♡ 9 8 5 3
                    ♢ 6 5
                    ♣ 6 4
♠ 8 4 3                              ♠ Q J 9
♡ J 7              ┌─────────┐       ♡ Q 10 6 2
♢ A J 10 7 3 2    │    N    │       ♢ 8 4
♣ 10 2            │ W     E │       ♣ J 8 7 5
                  │    S    │
                  └─────────┘
                    ♠ K 7
                    ♡ A K 4
                    ♢ K Q 9
                    ♣ A K Q 9 3
```

West	North	East	South
			2♣
pass	2♢	pass	3NT
all pass			

The Bidding: South rebids 3NT, showing 24-25 HCPs. North holds a precious ace but this is not enough to contemplate a slam.

The Play: How will you play 3NT when West leads the ♢J and East plays the ♢4?

You win with the ♢Q and count eight top tricks, including one diamond already won. You therefore need just one extra trick to bring you the game. You must try to create this extra trick without allowing East on lead. Otherwise a diamond from East through your ♢K9 may be fatal.

If clubs are 3-3 you will have two extra tricks there. You would like to make 3NT when clubs break 4-2, though. If West held four clubs, it would be simple enough to play the top three clubs and concede a trick to West, the safe hand who cannot continue diamonds effectively. It's much more likely that East, who is short in diamonds, will hold the club length.

At Trick 2 you should lead the ♣7 to dummy's ♠A and then lead a club, finessing the ♣9. West (the safe hand) will win with the ♣10 and cannot do you any damage in diamonds. When you regain the lead, four club tricks and the contract will be yours. This technique is known as ducking a trick into the safe hand.

REVERSES

Look carefully at the following starts to an auction:

A.	**You**	**Partner**	**B.**	**You**	**Partner**
	1♦	1♥		1♣	1♥
	2♣			2♦	

In sequence A, you may hold a minimum opening bid; if your partner prefers diamonds to clubs, he can rebid 2♦ and the bidding may stop there. Sequence B is subtly different. If partner prefers your first suit, he will have to go to 3♣.

The 2♦ rebid is known as a reverse. Because it may force the bidding quite high, even when responder holds no extra values, a reverse shows extra strength. Usually you will hold at least 17 HCP for such a bid. Note that the suit that you bid first must be longer than your second suit. You might hold this hand for sequence B:

♠ A 10 8   ♥ 6   ♦ K Q 9 2   ♣ A K J 7 6

A reverse facing a one-level response is forcing for one round. Facing a two-level response, a reverse is forcing to game.

What do you do when you have the right shape for a reverse but not enough HCP? You may then have to rebid your first suit:

♠ 6 4   ♥ K 5   ♦ A J 8 4   ♣ K Q 10 8 5

You	Partner
1♣	1♠
2♣	

Not strong enough to reverse, you rebid 2♣. (An alternative is 1NT, showing 12-14 points and a balanced hand.)

Suppose the bidding starts 1♦ – 1♠ – 2♥, where the opener has reversed. What options does the responder have when he is weak and does not want to bid to the game-level? He may rebid his own suit at the minimum level (2♠), bid notrump at the minimum level (2NT) or give preference to the opener's first suit (3♦). After anything else, the bidding must continue to game.

PLAY DEAL 5-1

Both Vul. Dealer North

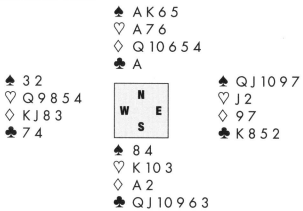

```
                    ♠ A K 6 5
                    ♡ A 7 6
                    ◇ Q 10 6 5 4
                    ♣ A
  ♠ 3 2                              ♠ Q J 10 9 7
  ♡ Q 9 8 5 4          N             ♡ J 2
  ◇ K J 8 3        W       E         ◇ 9 7
  ♣ 7 4                S             ♣ K 8 5 2
                    ♠ 8 4
                    ♡ K 10 3
                    ◇ A 2
                    ♣ Q J 10 9 6 3
```

West	North	East	South
	1◇	pass	2♣
pass	2♠	pass	2NT
pass	3NT	all pass	

The Bidding: With 17 HCP, North is strong enough to rebid 2♠ — a reverse bid. This is forcing to game opposite a two-level response, so South can rebid just 2NT rather than 3NT. North has no more distribution to show and raises to 3NT.

The Play: How would you play 3NT when West leads the ♡5? It may seem tempting to run the lead into your ♡K10 but this will cost the contract! East's ♡J will force your ♡K and you will not have enough entries to establish and enjoy your splendid club suit. (If you play low from dummy and allow the ♡J to win, East has the chance to remove your ◇A entry with a ◇9 switch.)

Before playing to the first trick, you should make a plan for the contract. You start with six top tricks and can easily make the extra tricks that you need by setting up the clubs. To preserve the entries to your hand, you should win the first trick with dummy's ♡A. You then play the ♣A and reach your hand with the ◇A. You lead the ♣Q to set up the suit and the defenders are powerless. If East wins with the ♣K and returns a heart, you will win with the ♡K and score four more club tricks. An overtrick is yours.

PLAY DEAL 5-2

Both Vul. Dealer South

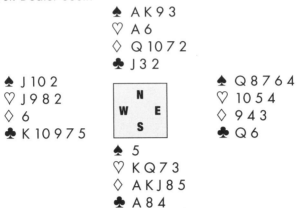

```
                    ♠ A K 9 3
                    ♡ A 6
                    ◇ Q 10 7 2
                    ♣ J 3 2
  ♠ J 10 2                              ♠ Q 8 7 6 4
  ♡ J 9 8 2          N                  ♡ 10 5 4
  ◇ 6            W       E              ◇ 9 4 3
  ♣ K 10 9 7 5        S                 ♣ Q 6
                    ♠ 5
                    ♡ K Q 7 3
                    ◇ A K J 8 5
                    ♣ A 8 4
```

West	North	East	South
			1◇
pass	1♠	pass	2♡
pass	4◇	pass	4NT
pass	5♡	pass	6◇
all pass			

The Bidding: When North hears a reverse from partner, promising at least a five-card diamond suit, he can visualize a slam in that suit. He leaps to 4◇, not in the least worried that will go past 3NT. South bids Blackwood and partner's 5♡ response shows two aces. (If the partnership were playing Roman Keycard Blackwood — see Chapter 20 — North would respond 5♠ to show two aces and the ◇Q.) South's 6◇ ends the auction.

The Play: How would you play 6◇ when West leads the ♠J? You can count eleven top tricks and a heart ruff will bring the total to twelve. When both defenders follow to the first round of trumps, there is no reason not to draw all the remaining trumps. You play three top hearts and ruff your last heart in dummy. You can then discard one of your two club losers on the ♠K and claim the slam.

PLAY DEAL 5-3

Both Vul. Dealer South

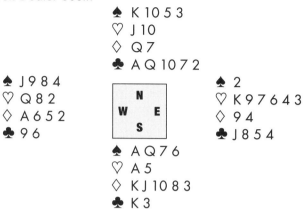

```
              ♠ K 10 5 3
              ♡ J 10
              ◇ Q 7
              ♣ A Q 10 7 2
♠ J 9 8 4                      ♠ 2
♡ Q 8 2          N            ♡ K 9 7 6 4 3
◇ A 6 5 2      W   E          ◇ 9 4
♣ 9 6            S            ♣ J 8 5 4
              ♠ A Q 7 6
              ♡ A 5
              ◇ K J 10 8 3
              ♣ K 3
```

West	North	East	South
			1◇
pass	2♣	pass	2♠
pass	3♠	pass	4NT
pass	5◇	pass	6♠
all pass			

The Bidding: North is strong enough to make two bids and correctly bids the clubs first, intending to bid spades next. South reverses into 2♠, which is game-forcing opposite a two-level response. North agrees spades and South bids 4NT to ask for aces (see Chapter 6). On discovering that an ace is missing, South signs off in 6♠.

The Play: Imagine you are West now and try to forget any cards that you have seen, looking only at the bidding. What opening lead would you choose?

The original West thought: 'I have a very likely trump trick, so I'd better play my ◇A before the rats get at it.' He led the ◇A and continued with another diamond. Declarer then had an easy ride. He played the ace and queen of trumps, East showing out on the second round, and then took a marked finesse of the ♠10. After drawing the last trump, he claimed the contract. He would score four trumps, four diamonds, three clubs and the ♡A.

A heart lead (the unbid suit) would have defeated the slam. As the cards lie, declarer could not then avoid losing a heart and a diamond.

PLAY DEAL 5-4

Both Vul. Dealer North

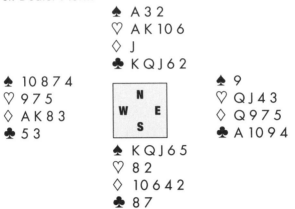

```
                    ♠ A 3 2
                    ♡ A K 10 6
                    ◇ J
                    ♣ K Q J 6 2
     ♠ 10 8 7 4                      ♠ 9
     ♡ 9 7 5           N            ♡ Q J 4 3
     ◇ A K 8 3    W        E        ◇ Q 9 7 5
     ♣ 5 3             S            ♣ A 10 9 4
                    ♠ K Q J 6 5
                    ♡ 8 2
                    ◇ 10 6 4 2
                    ♣ 8 7
```

West	North	East	South
	1♣	pass	1♠
pass	2♡	pass	2♠
pass	4♠	all pass	

The Bidding: With 18 HCP, North is happy to reverse to 2♡ (forcing for one round opposite a one-level response). South rebids his spades and North then jumps to 4♠, hoping to lose no more than one trump and two tricks in the side suits.

The Play: For the moment, look just at the West cards and the North-South bidding. What would you lead against 4♠?

An ace-king combination is normally a great lead and you would reach quickly for one of the top diamonds. Here, though, it is very likely from North's bidding that he has only one diamond (3=4=1=5 shape). The best lead is a trump and that would in fact have beaten the contract. Now take the South cards. How will you play 4♠ when West leads the ◇A and switches to the ♠4, East playing the ♠9?

You win with the ♠J and play a club to the king. If East holds up the ace, you play the ♣Q. On lead with the ♣A, East cannot beat you. If he plays the ♣10, you will discard a diamond and lose just one trump, one diamond and one club. If instead he returns a diamond, you will ruff in the dummy and play the ♣J yourself, throwing your penultimate diamond. West can ruff this, but now you will trump your last diamond in dummy with the ♠A (or if West returns a trump, you ruff a club high to get back to your hand, draw his last trump, and cross back to dummy to throw a diamond on the fifth club).

BLACKWOOD AND GERBER

The Blackwood convention uses a bid of 4NT to ask partner how many aces he holds. Let's say you have the following hand:

♠ A K 8 6 4   ♡ K Q 9 6 2   ◇ 7   ♣ K Q

You	Partner
1♠	2♡
4NT (Blackwood)	

You need to know how many aces partner holds. You want to be in 6♡ when he has two aces, 7♡ when he has three. If he disappoints you by showing one ace, you stop safely in 5♡. These are the responses to 4NT:

5♣	0 or 4 aces
5◇	1 ace
5♡	2 aces
5♠	3 aces

You should use Blackwood only when the previous bidding has convinced you that the partnership holds sufficient playing strength to score at least twelve tricks. Ideally, you should be confident that you do not have two quick losers in any suit. Remember that Blackwood is not a slam-try. It is last-moment check that you do not have two aces missing.

You may follow a Blackwood 4NT with 5NT to ask for kings. 6♣ will show 0 or 4 kings. 6◇, 6♡ and 6♠ will show 1, 2 and 3 kings respectively.

There are a few auctions where a 4NT bid is not Blackwood:

(1) You	Partner	(2) You	Partner
1NT (or 2NT)	4NT	1NT	2♣
		2♠	4NT

Partner's 4NT is a limit bid, inviting a slam. You may pass or raise to 6NT. If partner had wanted to ask for aces after either of these starts, he would bid 4♣ (the Gerber convention) instead. You would then respond 4◇ with 0 or 4 aces, 4♡ with one ace, 4♠ with two aces and 4NT with three aces.

PLAY DEAL 6-1

N-S Vul. Dealer South.

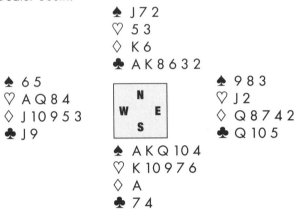

```
                    ♠ J 7 2
                    ♡ 5 3
                    ◇ K 6
                    ♣ A K 8 6 3 2
  ♠ 6 5                          ♠ 9 8 3
  ♡ A Q 8 4          N           ♡ J 2
  ◇ J 10 9 5 3    W     E        ◇ Q 8 7 4 2
  ♣ J 9              S           ♣ Q 10 5
                    ♠ A K Q 10 4
                    ♡ K 10 9 7 6
                    ◇ A
                    ♣ 7 4
```

West	North	East	South
			1♠
pass	2♣	pass	2♡
pass	3♠	pass	4NT
pass	5◇	pass	6♠
all pass			

The Bidding: South's 2♡ rebid is forcing opposite a two-level response. (There is absolutely no need to waste space by jumping to 3♡, even if your hand is stronger than this.) When South hears a two-level response and jump support of spades, he decides to bid 6♠ unless two aces are missing.

The Play: How will you play 6♠ when West leads the ◇J? Some players would lead a heart to the king at some stage, bemoaning their luck when West won with the ♡A and promptly cashed a second heart trick. It is better to hope that clubs are 3-2 and can be established with one ruff.

Should you draw trumps after winning with the ◇A? No, because you will need the ♠J as an entry to the established cards in the club suit. Play the ♠A and ♠K if you like. When the trumps break 3-2, you go ahead with your plan to set up the clubs. Both defenders follow to the first two rounds of the suit. You then ruff a third round of clubs — with a high trump to avoid a possible over-ruff. Finally, you return to dummy with the ♠J. You can then discard four of your hearts, one on the ◇K and another three on the established cards in clubs.

PLAY DEAL 6-2

E-W Vul. Dealer South.

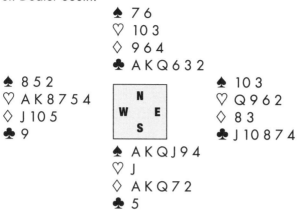

♠ 7 6
♡ 10 3
♢ 9 6 4
♣ A K Q 6 3 2

♠ 8 5 2
♡ A K 8 7 5 4
♢ J 10 5
♣ 9

♠ 10 3
♡ Q 9 6 2
♢ 8 3
♣ J 10 8 7 4

♠ A K Q J 9 4
♡ J
♢ A K Q 7 2
♣ 5

West	North	East	South
			2♣
pass	3♣	pass	3♠
pass	4♣	pass	4♢
pass	4♠	pass	4NT
pass	5♢	pass	6♠
all pass			

The Bidding: Spades are agreed as trumps and South decides he will bid a small slam if North has one ace, a grand slam if he has two aces. He bids 4NT and North's 5♢ response shows one ace. Right, 6♠ it is!

The Play: Take the West cards for a moment. Do you think you will be able to score two heart tricks? Only if South is completely mad. Anyway, you should lead the ♡K rather than the ♡A to ask partner to give you a count signal. This is standard practice when defending at the five-level or higher. East signals with the ♡9, showing four (or two) hearts, and South follows with the ♡J. West at the table made a smart switch to the ♣9, hoping to cut declarer off from the dummy. Quickly switch seats and take declarer's cards now. How will you play the small slam after winning with the ♣Q?

If clubs are 3-3, you can play the ♣AK and throw your two potential diamond losers. Otherwise you can draw trumps and hope for a 3-2 diamond break. (There is no point at all in trying to take just one more club trick because you have two low diamonds.) Drawing trumps and playing for a 3-2 diamond break is easily the best chance. This line of play lands the slam.

Neither Vul. Dealer North.

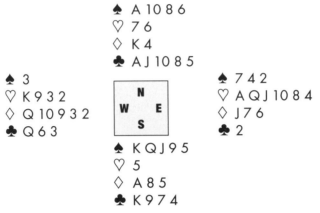

♠ A 10 8 6
♡ 7 6
◇ K 4
♣ A J 10 8 5

♠ 3
♡ K 9 3 2
◇ Q 10 9 3 2
♣ Q 6 3

♠ 7 4 2
♡ A Q J 10 8 4
◇ J 7 6
♣ 2

♠ K Q J 9 5
♡ 5
◇ A 8 5
♣ K 9 7 4

West	North	East	South
	1♣	2♡	2♠
4♡	4♠	pass	4NT
pass	5♡	pass	6♠
all pass			

The Bidding: When South hears of a double fit in the black suits, he decides to play in a small slam provided there are not two aces missing. North's 5♡ response confirms that this is not the case and he leaps to 6♠.

The Play: How will you play 6♠ when West leads the ♡2 to the ♡A and East continues with the ♡Q?

You ruff the second heart and draw trumps. You then need to pick up the clubs without loss. How will you set about that task? Whenever you have a critical guess in one suit, you should seek information about the other suits. Your aim is to obtain a complete count on the defenders' hands.

It is very likely that East began with six hearts and he has shown up with three spades. If you can discover how many diamonds he has, you will know how the club suit lies. You play the ◇K and ◇A and ruff a diamond in dummy. East follows three times, so he has space for at most one club in his hand (his shape is either 3=6=3=1 or 3=6=4=0). You play the ♣K and see that East's only club is the ♣2. On the next round you finesse dummy's ♣J and the finesse wins, as you knew it would. The slam is yours. If East had begun with only two diamonds, showing out on the third round, his shape would have been 3=6=2=2 and you would have played for the drop in clubs.

PLAY DEAL 6-4

Both Vul. Dealer South.

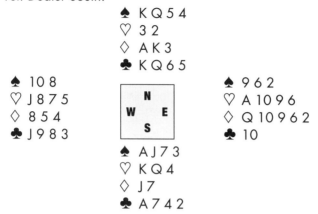

                    ♠ K Q 5 4
                    ♡ 3 2
                    ♢ A K 3
                    ♣ K Q 6 5
    ♠ 10 8   ♠ 9 6 2
    ♡ J 8 7 5   N   ♡ A 10 9 6
    ♢ 8 5 4   W   E   ♢ Q 10 9 6 2
    ♣ J 9 8 3   S   ♣ 10
                    ♠ A J 7 3
                    ♡ K Q 4
                    ♢ J 7
                    ♣ A 7 4 2

West	North	East	South
			1NT
pass	2♣	pass	2♠
pass	4♣	pass	4♠
pass	6♠	all pass	

The Bidding: When North locates a spade fit, he decides to play in 6♠ rather than 6NT. The opponents might hold 8 HCPs, so he needs to check that they do not hold two aces. A rebid of 4NT would not be Blackwood, it would be a quantitative bid inviting a slam. He therefore bids 4♣, Gerber. South's 4♠ response shows two aces and North then bids 6♠.

The Play: How will you play 6♠ when West leads the ♢8?

You can restrict your heart losers to just one, even if West holds the ♡A, by ruffing the third round of hearts in dummy. The main risk to the contract is that clubs are 4-1 and that you will have a loser in that suit. You can attempt to overcome a bad club break by leading twice towards the ♡KQ4. If East happens to hold the ♡A, you will discard a club from dummy on the third round of hearts.

You win with the ♢A, draw trumps in three rounds and lead a heart to the ♡K. When this wins, you return to dummy with the ♢K and lead a second round of hearts towards your hand. If East rises with the ♡A, you will have a discard for dummy's fourth club and can subsequently ruff a club in dummy. If East chooses to play low on the second round of hearts, you will win with the queen, ruff a heart and lose just one club trick.

7

NEGATIVE DOUBLES

A negative double is used when partner opens the bidding with one of a suit and your right-hand opponent overcalls in a suit at a low level. Such a double is for takeout, with emphasis on any unbid major(s).

LHO	Partner	RHO	You
	1◇	1♠	dbl

You guarantee four cards in hearts, the unbid major. You will usually also hold four cards in one of the minors. At the one-level you need no more than 6 points to make a negative double:

(1) ♠ 8 7 3
   ♡ A J 7 6
   ◇ Q 7
   ♣ 10 9 5 4

(2) ♠ J 7
   ♡ K Q 10 2
   ◇ A 8 7 4
   ♣ K 9 3

Hand (1) represents a near-minimum negative double over 1♠. You would start with a double on (2) as well, intending to drive the bidding to game. As the level of RHO's overcall increases, the more points you need for a negative double. To double after an overcall of 2♠, you would need at least a 10-count.

The opener rebids naturally, giving an indication of his overall strength.

You
♠ A 6
♡ K J 7 2
◇ A Q 10 5 4
♣ Q 7

You	LHO	Partner	RHO
1◇	1♠	dbl	pass
3♡			

Partner indicates hearts with his negative double. With a minimum opening and this shape, you would rebid 2♡. Here you make it 3♡. With a good picture of your strength, partner can judge whether a game is possible.

Playing negative doubles means that you cannot double for penalties when you are strong in RHO's suit. With such a hand you must pass initially, hoping that partner will reopen with a (takeout) double. You can then leave this in for penalties.

PLAY DEAL 7-1

Both Vul. Dealer South.

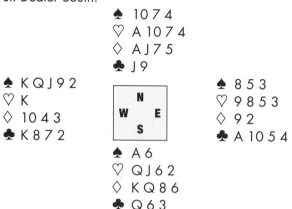

```
                    ♠ 10 7 4
                    ♡ A 10 7 4
                    ◇ A J 7 5
                    ♣ J 9
    ♠ K Q J 9 2                      ♠ 8 5 3
    ♡ K              N               ♡ 9 8 5 3
    ◇ 10 4 3      W     E            ◇ 9 2
    ♣ K 8 7 2        S               ♣ A 10 5 4
                    ♠ A 6
                    ♡ Q J 6 2
                    ◇ K Q 8 6
                    ♣ Q 6 3
```

West	North	East	South
			1◇
1♠	dbl	pass	2♡
pass	3♡	pass	4♡
all pass			

The Bidding: North has enough points to bid over 1♠ but no good natural bid to make. He doesn't want to raise diamonds immediately in case he misses a 4-4 heart fit. He starts with a negative double and is happy to hear South bid hearts. What next? With 10 points he is just about worth a raise to 3♡, inviting a game. South accepts and the heart game is reached.

The Play: How would you play 4♡ when West leads the ♠K? You win with the ace and decide to draw trumps. Will you lead the ♡Q or a low heart? As the cards lie, it will cost you the contract if you lead the queen. This will be covered by the king and dummy's ace. Since the ♡J and ♡10 are your only remaining trump honors, East will score a trick with his ♡985. You will lose two clubs, one spade and a trump, going one down.

Instead, you should lead a low heart to the ♡10 on the first round. When West's ♡K appears, you win with the ♡A and the suit is yours without loss.

Should you draw all the trumps now? No, because you would make only nine tricks (four trumps, four diamonds and the ♠A). Instead you should give up a spade trick. When you win the return, you can ruff a spade in your hand, draw the remaining trumps and claim the contract. You will then make a total of five trump tricks, and ten tricks in all.

PLAY DEAL 7-2

Neither Vul. Dealer North.

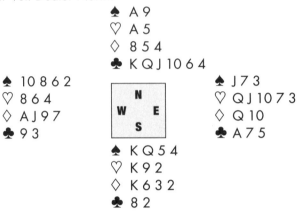

```
                    ♠ A 9
                    ♡ A 5
                    ◇ 8 5 4
                    ♣ K Q J 10 6 4
   ♠ 10 8 6 2              N          ♠ J 7 3
   ♡ 8 6 4          W            E    ♡ Q J 10 7 3
   ◇ A J 9 7               S          ◇ Q 10
   ♣ 9 3                              ♣ A 7 5
                    ♠ K Q 5 4
                    ♡ K 9 2
                    ◇ K 6 3 2
                    ♣ 8 2
```

West	North	East	South
	1♣	1♡	dbl
2♡	3♣	pass	3NT
all pass			

The Bidding: East overcalls 1♡ and South makes a negative double. (If he held five spades, he would respond 1♠ instead.) West has enough to raise to 2♡ and North rebids 3♣. South expects his partner to have something beyond a minimum opening bid for his rebid and tries his luck in 3NT.

The Play: West leads the ♡8 and declarer wins with dummy's ace, continuing with the ♣K. East ducks the first two rounds of clubs and wins the third round, his partner discarding the ♡4. East can count five club tricks for declarer along with the ♡A, ♡K and ♠A. If South holds the ◇A he will have at least nine tricks and the game will be unbeatable. The best chance for the defenders is that four diamond tricks can now be taken. How should declarer play when East switches to the ◇Q?

If South mistakenly covers the first round of diamonds with the king, West will win and claim three more tricks in the suit for one down. The same fate will await declarer if he covers the ◇10 on the second round. He therefore ducks again and East has no further diamond to play. When he returns some other suit, declarer will claim the remaining tricks, scoring an overtrick. After this accurate play by declarer, the best the defenders can do is for West to overtake the ◇10 with the ◇J and then cash the ◇A, holding declarer to nine tricks.

PLAY DEAL 7-3

Both Vul. Dealer South.

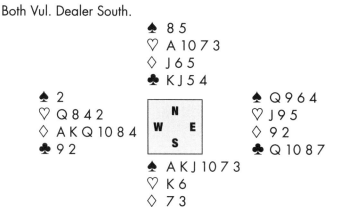

```
                    ♠ 8 5
                    ♡ A 10 7 3
                    ♢ J 6 5
                    ♣ K J 5 4
♠ 2                                      ♠ Q 9 6 4
♡ Q 8 4 2          N                     ♡ J 9 5
♢ A K Q 10 8 4   W   E                   ♢ 9 2
♣ 9 2              S                     ♣ Q 10 8 7
                    ♠ A K J 10 7 3
                    ♡ K 6
                    ♢ 7 3
                    ♣ A 6 3
```

West	North	East	South
			1♠
2♢	dbl	pass	3♠
pass	4♠	all pass	

The Bidding: North has enough points for a negative double over 2♢. South is going to rebid his spades, but at what level? Correctly, he decides to bid 3♠ rather than 2♠. Knowing of good spades and extra values opposite, North raises to 4♠.

The Play: How would you play 4♠ when West leads out the three top diamonds, East discarding the ♡5 on the third round?

You ruff in your hand and pause to calculate the best play in the trump suit. You are going to finesse against the ♠Q, yes, but should you cash the ♠A on the first round in case West holds a singleton ♠Q? No. This play would gain if West held a singleton ♠Q, but it would lose four times as often when West held a singleton 9, 6, 4 or 2 in the suit.

You lead the ♡6 to dummy's ace and finesse the ♠J. It wins (hurray!). What are you going to do next? Will you play the ♠A and ♠K, hoping that East began with ♠Qxx? It is better to repeat the trump finesse, so you can pick up ♠Qxxx with East. With this in mind, you lead a club to the jack. The finesse loses but on any return you will be able to cross to dummy with the ♣K and finesse the ♠10. You can then draw trumps and claim the contract.

PLAY DEAL 7-4

Neither Vul. Dealer South.

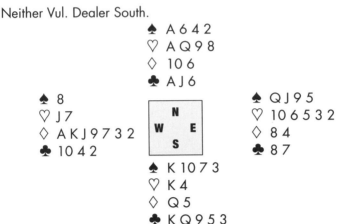

```
                    ♠ A 6 4 2
                    ♡ A Q 9 8
                    ◇ 10 6
                    ♣ A J 6
   ♠ 8                              ♠ Q J 9 5
   ♡ J 7           N                ♡ 10 6 5 3 2
   ◇ A K J 9 7 3 2  W   E           ◇ 8 4
   ♣ 10 4 2          S              ♣ 8 7
                    ♠ K 10 7 3
                    ♡ K 4
                    ◇ Q 5
                    ♣ K Q 9 5 3
```

West	North	East	South
			1♣
3◇	dbl	pass	3♠
pass	4♠	all pass	

The Bidding: West overcalls 3◇ and North makes a negative double, hoping to find a 4-4 fit in a major suit. South has a fit for spades and bids only 3♠ (rather than 4♠) because his hand is in the minimum range. North is strong enough to advance to 4♠.

The Play: West leads two top diamonds, everyone following. From his point of view, the best chance of beating the contract is that East's expected four trumps will yield two defensive tricks. Although it's normally a bad idea to give a ruff-and-sluff, West cleverly realizes that this may cause a problem for declarer, forcing him to ruff in one hand or another. Take the South cards now. How will you play the contract when West leads the ◇J at Trick 3?

If you ruff in the South hand, you will go down. East is likely to hold four trumps, so you should keep your ♠K1073 intact. You ruff with dummy's ♠2 and East discards a club. What now? You play dummy's ♠A and West follows with the ♠8. Your aim now is to finesse your ♠10. If trumps are 3-2 and West wins the trick, you will make the contract easily. If East plays the ♠9 on the second round, you finesse the ♠10 and lose only one trump trick. If instead East inserts the ♠J, you win with the ace. You will then return to dummy with a heart to lead towards the ♠10 on the third round.

JACOBY AND TEXAS TRA

Jacoby transfers are used opposite an opening bid of 1NT. ~~~~
cards in a major suit, you respond in the suit below the one you hold:

Partner	You
1NT	2◊ (transfer to hearts)
2♡	

Partner	You
1NT	2♡ (transfer to spades)
2♠	

The responder can then either pass, if his hand is weak, or advance with a game bid or game try. There are three big advantages of this scheme:

1. **The strong hand is concealed from the defenders** since the opening bidder becomes declarer, making the defense more difficult.
2. **The opening lead comes up to the strong hand** and declarer will often gain a trick as a result.
3. **The responder gets a second bid** and this greatly increases the number of bidding sequences that are available.

Suppose the bidding starts 1NT – 2♡ – 2♠. When responder has only five spades and 10+ points, he may continue with 3NT to ask partner to choose between 3NT and 4♠. The opener should choose spades with at least three-card support. If instead responder is worth only a game try, he may bid 2NT instead. The opener then has four options: pass or 3♠ when lower-range, 3NT or 4♠ when upper-range. With a strong hand the responder may also bid a new suit (1NT – 2◊ – 2♡ – 3♣), which is forcing to game.

Jacoby transfers are used also after a 2NT opening (or 2♣ – 2◊ – 2NT). A response of 3◊ shows 5+ hearts; 3♡ shows 5+ spades.

Texas transfers are used with a major suit of 6+ cards when responder wants to be in game (and perhaps to shut out the opponents from a good sacrifice). 1NT – 4◊ asks partner to bid 4♡. 1NT – 4♡ requests a 4♠ rebid.

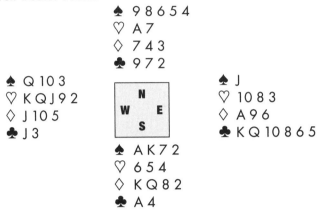

♠ 9 8 6 5 4
♡ A 7
♢ 7 4 3
♣ 9 7 2

♠ Q 10 3   ♠ J
♡ K Q J 9 2   ♡ 10 8 3
♢ J 10 5   ♢ A 9 6
♣ J 3   ♣ K Q 10 8 6 5

♠ A K 7 2
♡ 6 5 4
♢ K Q 8 2
♣ A 4

West	North	East	South
			1NT
pass	2♡	pass	2♠
pass	pass	3♣	3♠
all pass			

The Bidding: North transfers into spades, hoping that 2♠ will play better than 1NT. When South's 2♠ bid runs to East, he decides to contest the auction, bidding 3♣. Although North has not promised any values at all, South has excellent trump support and several useful cards. He allows himself to be pushed to 3♠, which becomes the final contract.

The Play: How will you play 3♠ when West leads the ♡K?

As always, you look at the losers in the long-trump hand (North here). You can see one heart, two diamonds and two clubs. If trumps are 3-1, there will be a loser in that suit too. You can ruff a club loser in the South hand. You should aim to lead twice towards your diamond honors, hoping that East holds the ♢A. What will you do at Trick 2 after winning with the ♡A?

Dummy is very short of entries and you should lead a diamond towards your hand while you have the chance. The ♢K wins and you play the ♠AK, finding that you have a trump loser. When you give up a round of hearts, West wins and draws a third round of trumps. That's no problem. On any return, you will be able to ruff a heart in dummy and lead towards the ♢Q. You will lose one trick in each suit, making the contract.

PLAY DEAL 8-2

Neither Vul. Dealer South.

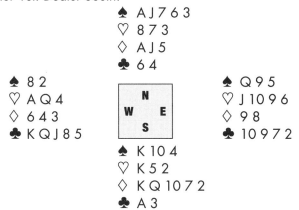

```
                      ♠ A J 7 6 3
                      ♡ 8 7 3
                      ◇ A J 5
                      ♣ 6 4
    ♠ 8 2                              ♠ Q 9 5
    ♡ A Q 4          ┌─────────┐      ♡ J 10 9 6
    ◇ 6 4 3          │    N    │      ◇ 9 8
    ♣ K Q J 8 5      │  W   E  │      ♣ 10 9 7 2
                     │    S    │
                     └─────────┘
                      ♠ K 10 4
                      ♡ K 5 2
                      ◇ K Q 10 7 2
                      ♣ A 3
```

West	North	East	South
			1NT
pass	2♡	pass	2♠
pass	3NT	pass	4♠
all pass			

The Bidding: North responds with a Jacoby 2♡, showing at least five spades. South rebids 2♠, as requested, and North's 3NT continuation says: 'I have only five spades. Please choose between 4♠ and 3NT.' With three-card spade support, South chooses 4♠ as the final contract.

The Play: When West leads the ♣K, you should hold up the ♣A on the first round and win the club continuation. You then need to draw trumps. Suppose you play the ♠K and finesse the ♠J. This will lose to the ♠Q and East's switch to the ♡J will give the defenders three heart tricks for one down. What was wrong with that line of play? It would be finessing into the danger hand (East is the danger hand, since he can put the contract at risk by switching to a heart through your ♡K).

A better idea is to cross to the ♠A and then finesse the ♠10 into the safe (West) hand. Even if the finesse loses to the ♠Q with West, you will still make the contract. West will not be able to underlead his club honors (crossing to the East hand for a heart switch) because of your hold-up at Trick 1. When you regain the lead, you will draw trumps and discard hearts from dummy on your diamond suit.

PLAY DEAL 8-3

Both Vul. Dealer South.

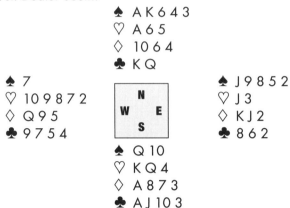

♠ A K 6 4 3
♡ A 6 5
◇ 10 6 4
♣ K Q

♠ 7
♡ 10 9 8 7 2
◇ Q 9 5
♣ 9 7 5 4

♠ J 9 8 5 2
♡ J 3
◇ K J 2
♣ 8 6 2

♠ Q 10
♡ K Q 4
◇ A 8 7 3
♣ A J 10 3

West	North	East	South
			1NT
pass	2♡	pass	2♠
pass	4NT	pass	6NT
all pass			

The Bidding: North responds with a Jacoby 2♡, showing at least five spades. South rebids 2♠, as requested. What do you think North's 4NT continuation means? It is not any form of Blackwood because no suit has been agreed. It is a non-forcing quantitative bid, inviting a slam. (You will recall that 2NT would also be non-forcing, inviting a game.) South decides to accept the try. He bids 6NT, rather than 6♠, because he does not have good support for spades. With three or more spades, South would have bid 6♠.

The Play: How should you play 6NT when West leads the ♡10? You have eleven top tricks and have avoided a potentially awkward diamond lead. If spades are 3-3, you will have 13 easy tricks. If spades are 4-2, you can afford to give up a spade trick and still make 6NT. The only risk is that spades will break 5-1. How can you give yourself the best chance in that case?

Suppose you win the heart lead and play a spade to the queen. You will succeed against a 5-1 spade break only when a defender has a singleton ♠J. It is much better to win the heart lead in dummy and then finesse the ♠10. You will then succeed when West's spade singleton is the 9, 8, 7, 5 or 2.

PLAY DEAL 8-4

Both Vul. Dealer North.

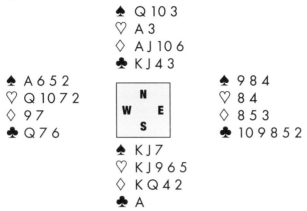

```
                    ♠ Q 10 3
                    ♡ A 3
                    ♢ A J 10 6
                    ♣ K J 4 3
   ♠ A 6 5 2                        ♠ 9 8 4
   ♡ Q 10 7 2        N              ♡ 8 4
   ♢ 9 7          W     E           ♢ 8 5 3
   ♣ Q 7 6           S              ♣ 10 9 8 5 2
                    ♠ K J 7
                    ♡ K J 9 6 5
                    ♢ K Q 4 2
                    ♣ A
```

West	North	East	South
	1NT	pass	2♢
pass	2♡	pass	3♢
pass	4♢	pass	4NT
pass	5♡	pass	6♢
all pass			

The Bidding: South shows his hearts with a 2♢ transfer response. Over the expected 2♡, he makes the game-forcing natural continuation of 3♢. North is happy to raise the diamonds and South advances to 6♢ after checking for aces.

The Play: 6♢ is a better contract than 6NT, since you have the chance to score one or more ruffing tricks. How would you play the slam when West leads the ♢7?

Once you have established two spade tricks, you will have ten tricks on top. If you can score two club ruffs in your hand, this will bring the total to twelve. You win the trump lead with the queen and play the ♣A. A spade to the ten wins the next trick and you ruff a club in your hand. Returning to dummy with the ♡A, you ruff a third round of clubs with the ♢K. You then draw trumps in two more rounds and knock out the ♠A. Twelve tricks are yours.

MORE

2

COMPLICATED

— FORCING MAJOR RAISE

_♡, or 1♠ to 3♠, this is a limit raise, showing _♡ and 10-12 points. When you have 13+ points with _♠ support, you use the Jacoby 2NT response. The alternative sequence of 1♡ – 4♡ shows a 'weak freak', around 6-9 points and at least five-card support. After 1♠ – 2NT, the opener rebids on these lines:

3♣/3♢/3♡	singleton (or void) in the bid suit
3♠	16+ points, good trumps, no singleton or void
4♣/4♢/4♡	second suit of 5+ cards (two of three top honors)
3NT	16+ points, moderate trumps, no singleton or void
4♠	minimum, no singleton or void

Partner	You	Partner	You
♠ A 2	♠ K 5 3		1♡
♡ A 10 9 4	♡ K Q J 6 3	2NT	3♢
♢ 9 7 4 3	♢ 6		
♣ K Q 4	♣ A J 5 2		

Partner's hand fits splendidly with your singleton. He will head for a slam.

Partner	You	Partner	You
♠ A 2	♠ K 5 3		1♡
♡ A 10 9 4	♡ K Q J 6 3	2NT	3♢
♢ K Q 4	♢ 6		
♣ 9 7 4 3	♣ A J 5 2		

Now the ◇KQ are wasted and partner will sign off in 4♡.

Partner	You	Partner	You
♠ A J 5	♠ 8		1♡
♡ A 9 6 2	♡ K Q 10 8 7 3	2NT	4♣
♢ 10 8 7 3	♢ 6	4♠	4NT
♣ K 4	♣ A Q 10 8 3	5♡	6♡

With a fitting ♣K, partner cuebids 4♠ (see Chapter 14). Since you have a diamond control, you ask for aces and bid the small slam.

PLAY DEAL 9-1

Neither Vul. Dealer South.

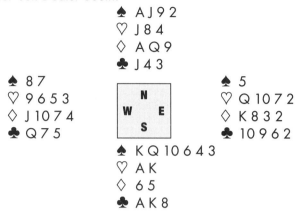

```
                    ♠ A J 9 2
                    ♡ J 8 4
                    ◇ A Q 9
                    ♣ J 4 3
    ♠ 8 7                           ♠ 5
    ♡ 9 6 5 3          N            ♡ Q 10 7 2
    ◇ J 10 7 4      W     E         ◇ K 8 3 2
    ♣ Q 7 5            S            ♣ 10 9 6 2
                    ♠ K Q 10 6 4 3
                    ♡ A K
                    ◇ 6 5
                    ♣ A K 8
```

West	North	East	South
			1♠
pass	2NT	pass	3♠
pass	4◇	pass	4♡
pass	4♠	pass	6♠
all pass			

The Bidding: North responds with a Jacoby 2NT. With a semi-balanced hand (no singleton or void) and good trumps, South rebids 3♠. Since the South hand is still unlimited, North cuebids his ◇A. South is now going to bid a small slam, at least. He cuebids in hearts and leaps to 6♠ when his partner attempts to sign off in 4♠.

The Play: West leads the ♠8, East following suit. How will you play 6♠?

You win with the ♠10 and draw the last trump with the ♠K. Your next move is to play the two top hearts, just in case (yes, it's a tiny chance) the ♡Q will fall in two rounds. This chance fails and you must now seek a second diamond trick on which you can throw your club loser. How should you play the diamonds to maximize your prospects?

If you finesse the ◇Q on the first round, you will have only a 50% chance of success. It is better to finesse the ◇9 on the first round. This will give you your twelfth trick immediately if West holds both the ◇J and the ◇10 (as in the diagram). If instead the ◇9 lost to a middle honor with East, nothing would have been lost. You could still return to your hand and finesse the ◇Q on the second round. Two chances are better than one!

PLAY DEAL 9-2

Neither Vul. Dealer South.

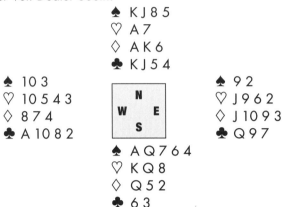

```
                    ♠ K J 8 5
                    ♡ A 7
                    ◇ A K 6
                    ♣ K J 5 4
  ♠ 10 3                            ♠ 9 2
  ♡ 10 5 4 3         N              ♡ J 9 6 2
  ◇ 8 7 4        W       E          ◇ J 10 9 3
  ♣ A 10 8 2         S              ♣ Q 9 7
                    ♠ A Q 7 6 4
                    ♡ K Q 8
                    ◇ Q 5 2
                    ♣ 6 3
```

West	North	East	South
			1♠
pass	2NT	pass	4♠
pass	4NT	pass	5◇
pass	6♠	all pass	

The Bidding: North bids a Jacoby 2NT. South shows a minimum opening with no singleton or void with his 4♠ response. Wild horses will not keep North out of a slam on his hand. He bids standard Blackwood, just in case two aces are missing. When partner shows an ace, he leaps to 6♠.

The Play: How will you play the slam when West leads the ◇8?
The hands fit disappointingly and, despite the magnificent dummy, you may have to guess the lie of the club suit. If West holds the ♣A, you will need to play a club to the king; if instead he holds the ♣Q, you will need to lead to the jack. When the club honors are split, you will have a 50-50 guess to make. Is there any way to bend the odds in your favor?
After winning the opening lead with the ◇Q, you should immediately lead the ♣3. When West holds the ♣A he may be caught unawares, perhaps expecting you to draw trumps first. If he plays the ♣A, or even thinks of doing so, he will give you the slam. If instead he plays low smoothly, you should finesse dummy's ♣J.
Many players would draw trumps first and maybe play one or both red suits next. This would tell the defenders that they need two club tricks.

PLAY DEAL 9-3

Neither Vul. Dealer South.

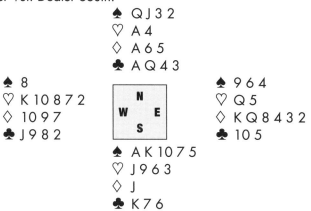

```
                    ♠ Q J 3 2
                    ♡ A 4
                    ◇ A 6 5
                    ♣ A Q 4 3
  ♠ 8                              ♠ 9 6 4
  ♡ K 10 8 7 2          N         ♡ Q 5
  ◇ 10 9 7          W       E      ◇ K Q 8 4 3 2
  ♣ J 9 8 2              S         ♣ 10 5
                    ♠ A K 10 7 5
                    ♡ J 9 6 3
                    ◇ J
                    ♣ K 7 6
```

West	North	East	South
			1♠
pass	2NT	pass	3◇
pass	4NT	pass	5♡
pass	5NT	pass	6♣
pass	6♠	all pass	

The Bidding: North responds with a Jacoby 2NT and South rebids 3◇ to show a diamond shortage. North uses Roman Keycard Blackwood (see Chapter 20) to locate the ♠AK and the ♣K. When he then bids 6♠, although North's 5NT announced that the partnership held the ♠AKQ and the three side-suit aces, South has no reason to bid any more.

The Play: How would you play the spade slam when West leads the ◇10? You begin with three potential heart losers and must aim to ruff two of them in the dummy. After winning with the ◇A, you should play ace and another heart. East wins with the ♡Q and returns the ◇K, which you ruff. You ruff a heart with dummy's ♠Q, return to your hand with the ♠A and ruff your last heart with the ♠J. You can then draw the remaining trumps and claim the contract.

By ruffing the two heart losers with high trumps, you avoid any risk of East overruffing.

PLAY DEAL 9-4

Neither Vul. Dealer South.

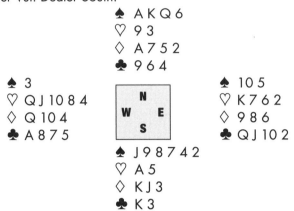

```
                        ♠ A K Q 6
                        ♡ 9 3
                        ◇ A 7 5 2
                        ♣ 9 6 4
    ♠ 3                                      ♠ 10 5
    ♡ Q J 10 8 4          N                  ♡ K 7 6 2
    ◇ Q 10 4          W       E              ◇ 9 8 6
    ♣ A 8 7 5              S                 ♣ Q J 10 2
                        ♠ J 9 8 7 4 2
                        ♡ A 5
                        ◇ K J 3
                        ♣ K 3
```

West	North	East	South
			1♠
pass	2NT	pass	4♠
all pass			

The Bidding: North responds with a Jacoby 2NT. Since South has a semi-balanced hand (no singleton or void), he must choose between three rebids: 3♠ non-minimum with good trumps, 3NT non-minimum with moderate trumps, or 4♠ minimum. It is close, but he chooses 4♠, ending the auction.

The Play: West leads the ♡Q, East signaling encouragement with the ♡7. Let's see first what happens if declarer wins the first trick with the ♡A. He draws trumps with the king and ace, continuing with a diamond to the jack. West wins with the ◇Q and crosses to partner's ♡K. A club switch then gives the defenders two more tricks for one down.

How can declarer do better? To prevent East from winning the lead (and switching to a club), it is essential to duck the first trick. You win the second round of hearts, draw trumps and finesse the ◇J. What a difference! West cannot now cross to partner's hand for a club switch. Nor can he effectively play clubs from his side of the table. On any continuation you will be able to discard a club on the thirteenth diamond.

Hold-ups are commonplace in notrump contracts. We see here that they can be equally useful in suit contracts. The objective is the same — to restrict the defenders' communications.

SPLINTER BIDS

A splinter bid is a double-jump in a new suit (for example, 1♠ – 4♣). It shows enough strength to bid game in partner's suit and at most one card in the splinter suit (clubs, here). These are all splinter bids:

Partner	You
1♠	4♣, 4◇ 4♡

Partner	You
1♡	3♠, 4♣, 4◇

A splinter bid is limited in strength. Slam should probably not be bid if partner has wasted honors in your short suit. These are the requirements to make one of the above splinter responses:

1. You have at least four-card support for partner's major,
2. You have 13-15 points (including distribution),
3. You have a singleton (not the ace or king) or void in the bid suit.

Here's a typical hand on which to respond 4♣ when partner opens 1♠:

♠ A 9 8 6 3   ♡ K Q 4   ◇ Q 9 8 3   ♣ 6

Suppose these are the two hands:

Partner	You
♠ K Q 10 7 2	♠ A 9 8 6 3
♡ A	♡ K Q 4
◇ A K 5 2	◇ Q 9 8 3
♣ 9 7 2	♣ 6

Partner sees that he can ruff clubs in your hand and will advance to 6♠.

The opener can use splinter bids too: 1◇ – 1♠ – 4♣. A rebid of 2♣ would be natural, perhaps a minimum hand. A rebid of 3♣ would be natural and very strong (game-forcing). So, a rebid of 4♣ is available as a splinter bid. It shows a sound raise to 4♠ (19+) including at most one club.

Neither Vul. Dealer South.

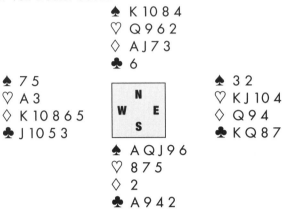

♠ K 10 8 4
♡ Q 9 6 2
◇ A J 7 3
♣ 6

♠ 7 5
♡ A 3
◇ K 10 8 6 5
♣ J 10 5 3

♠ 3 2
♡ K J 10 4
◇ Q 9 4
♣ K Q 8 7

♠ A Q J 9 6
♡ 8 7 5
◇ 2
♣ A 9 4 2

West	North	East	South
			1♠
pass	4♣	pass	4♠
all pass			

The Bidding: Although South holds only 11 HCP he is well worth an opening bid of 1♠. North is too strong for a raise to 3♠, since his singleton club may give South the chance of taking several spade ruffs in the dummy. He responds with a splinter bid of 4♣, showing his hand splendidly. Although South has the perfect club holding to face a singleton, he must sign off because his overall strength is minimum.

The Play: How will you play the spade game when West leads the ♠7, East following with the ♠2?

You win the trump lead and see that you can make a lot of tricks by ruffing in both hands. You have two side-suit winners (the minor-suit aces) and one trump trick already made. If you can add seven more trump tricks by ruffing in both hands, this will bring the total to ten.

You play the ♣A at Trick 2 and ruff a club in dummy. You then play the ◇A and ruff a diamond in your hand. Two more club ruffs in dummy and two more diamond ruffs in your hand bring the total to nine and the ♠A remains in your hand as the tenth trick.

Suppose you made the mistake of drawing a second round of trumps at the start. You would then go down. With only two club ruffs then possible in the dummy, you would be a trick short.

PLAY DEAL 10-2

Both Vul. Dealer South.

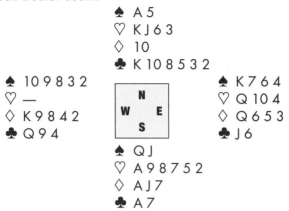

```
                    ♠ A 5
                    ♡ K J 6 3
                    ◊ 10
                    ♣ K 10 8 5 3 2
  ♠ 10 9 8 3 2                          ♠ K 7 6 4
  ♡ —             ┌─────────┐          ♡ Q 10 4
  ◊ K 9 8 4 2     │    N    │          ◊ Q 6 5 3
  ♣ Q 9 4         │ W     E │          ♣ J 6
                  │    S    │
                  └─────────┘
                    ♠ Q J
                    ♡ A 9 8 7 5 2
                    ◊ A J 7
                    ♣ A 7
```

West	North	East	South
			1♡
pass	4◊	pass	4NT
pass	5◊	pass	6♡
all pass			

The Bidding: North responds with a 4◊ splinter bid, showing 13-15 (including distribution), heart support and at most a singleton diamond. South sees that he will be able to ruff two diamonds in dummy. A small slam should have an excellent chance.

The Play: How will you play the heart slam when West leads the ♠10?
  The slam will be at risk only when East holds all three trumps and you have a loser in the suit. In that case, you cannot afford to lose a spade trick too. You should therefore not risk the slam by finessing in spades at Trick 1.
  You rise with the ♠A and play a trump to the ace. (East may decide to insert the ♡10 on this trick.) West shows out and you now have a trump loser. To dispose of your potential spade loser, you must establish dummy's club suit. When you play the ace and king of clubs, both defenders follow. You continue with a third round of clubs from dummy.
  If East were to ruff with the ♡Q, you would discard your spade loser. Let's say that he discards instead and you ruff in your hand. You play the ◊A and reach dummy with a diamond ruff. You then play a good club from dummy, discarding your spade loser as East ruffs. When he continues with the ♠K you ruff in your hand and claim the remaining tricks.

PLAY DEAL 10-3

Neither Vul. Dealer South.

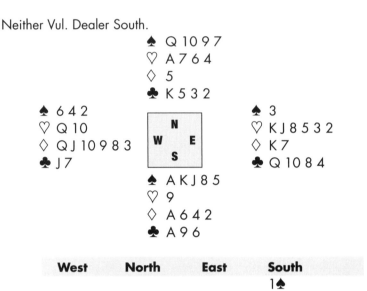

♠ Q 10 9 7
♡ A 7 6 4
◇ 5
♣ K 5 3 2

♠ 6 4 2
♡ Q 10
◇ Q J 10 9 8 3
♣ J 7

N
W E
S

♠ 3
♡ K J 8 5 3 2
◇ K 7
♣ Q 10 8 4

♠ A K J 8 5
♡ 9
◇ A 6 4 2
♣ A 9 6

West	North	East	South
			1♠
pass	4◇	pass	6♠
all pass			

The Bidding: When South hears of the perfect fit in diamonds (the ace opposite a singleton), he leaps to 6♠ without further ado. Bidding some form of Blackwood would be pointless, since he is willing to attempt twelve tricks whether or not the ♡A is missing.

The Play: How will you play the spade slam when West leads the ◇Q?

You win with the ◇A and see that you have four winners in the side suits. You will therefore need another eight tricks from the trump suit to bring the total to twelve. You can afford to draw one round of trumps, leading the ♠5 to the ♠Q. This leaves you with eight master trumps that you intend to score separately by ruffing diamonds in the dummy and hearts in your hand.

What will happen if you embark on this 'high crossruff' immediately? When you take the second heart ruff in your hand, West will discard one of his clubs. You will no longer be able to score two club tricks! It is therefore essential to play the ♣A and ♣K before crossruffing. With this business behind you, you ruff three hearts in your hand with the ♠8, ♠J and ♠K. Meanwhile, you ruff three diamonds in dummy with the ♠7, ♠9 and ♠10. Your ♣A will be the twelfth trick.

PLAY DEAL 10-4

E-W Vul. Dealer North.

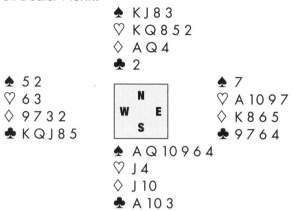

```
              ♠ K J 8 3
              ♡ K Q 8 5 2
              ◇ A Q 4
              ♣ 2
  ♠ 5 2                        ♠ 7
  ♡ 6 3          N             ♡ A 10 9 7
  ◇ 9 7 3 2   W     E          ◇ K 8 6 5
  ♣ K Q J 8 5    S             ♣ 9 7 6 4
              ♠ A Q 10 9 6 4
              ♡ J 4
              ◇ J 10
              ♣ A 10 3
```

West	North	East	South
	1♡	pass	1♠
pass	4♣	pass	4NT
pass	5♡	pass	6♠
all pass			

The Bidding: North decides that he is strong enough to bid game in spades. Rather than simply rebidding 4♠, he chooses 4♣ to show his shortage in that suit (a splinter bid by the opener). With six good trumps and an ace opposite partner's expected singleton, South heads for the small slam via Roman Keycard Blackwood.

The Play: Right, take the West cards first. What would you lead against 6♠ after the bidding shown?

Many players would look no further than the club sequence, perhaps recalling how well K-Q-J features on tables of approved opening leads. Here, though, North has advertised a singleton club. A club lead is safe but is it the best idea?

Let's assume that the ♣K is led. Take the South cards now. How will you play the slam?

You win with the ♣A, draw trumps in two rounds and lead the ♡J. This will set up a discard for your losing diamond and you can ruff your club losers in the dummy.

A diamond opening lead would have beaten the slam! Listen closely to the bidding and this will often help you to find the killing lead.

CUEBID RAISES

A bid of the opponent's suit when it cannot be natural is called a cuebid. One important use of such a bid is to show a good raise of partner's suit:

You	LHO	Partner	RHO	You
♠ A 2		1♡	2♣	3♣
♡ K 10 4 3				
◇ K 8 6 2				
♣ 9 7 4				

Your 3♣ shows at least a sound raise to 3♡, 10+ points. If instead you had bid 3♡ directly, this would be a preemptive (weak) raise based on four-card trump support and a bit of shape.

Your partner will rebid on the assumption that you have a minimum for your bid. He will rebid only 3♡ when his own hand is minimum. With a stronger hand he can bid 4♡ or even initiate some move towards a slam.

It is a huge advantage to be able to make two sorts of raise in partner's suit. You cuebid to investigate a game. When you raise partner's suit directly, your main aim is to remove bidding space from the opponents.

The same method is used when your partner has overcalled:

You	LHO	Partner	RHO	You
♠ K 8 4	1◇	1♠	pass	2◇
♡ A J 8 3				
◇ 5 3				
♣ K 10 7 2				

Your cuebid shows a sound raise based on HCP and support of 3+ cards.

You	LHO	Partner	RHO	You
♠ K Q J 5	1◇	1♠	pass	3♠
♡ 10 7 6				
◇ 5 2				
♣ 9 8 5 4				

Now you raise preemptively, to make life awkward for your LHO.

PLAY DEAL 11-1

N-S Vul. Dealer East

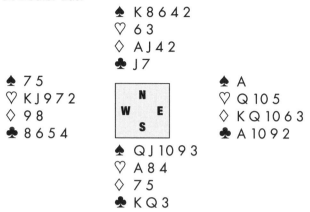

<table>
<tr><td></td><td>♠ K 8 6 4 2</td><td></td></tr>
<tr><td></td><td>♡ 6 3</td><td></td></tr>
<tr><td></td><td>◇ A J 4 2</td><td></td></tr>
<tr><td></td><td>♣ J 7</td><td></td></tr>
</table>

```
        ♠ K 8 6 4 2
        ♡ 6 3
        ◇ A J 4 2
        ♣ J 7
♠ 7 5              ♠ A
♡ K J 9 7 2    N   ♡ Q 10 5
◇ 9 8       W     E  ◇ K Q 10 6 3
♣ 8 6 5 4     S   ♣ A 10 9 2
        ♠ Q J 10 9 3
        ♡ A 8 4
        ◇ 7 5
        ♣ K Q 3
```

West	North	East	South
		1◇	1♠
pass	2◇	pass	3♠
pass	4♠	all pass	

The Bidding: Holding five-card support North would often raise directly to 4♠. This would be rather an overbid here, with no singleton in his hand, and North chooses to start by showing a sound raise to at least the two-level. South has values to spare for his one-level overcall and rebids 3♠ rather than 2♠. North is then happy to raise to game.

The Play: West leads the ◇9, giving you a chance. How will you play?

Suppose your first move after winning with the ◇A is to lead a trump. The defenders will then be able to set up a heart trick before you can take a discard on the clubs. You will lose one trick in each suit and go down. At Trick 2, you should lead the ♣J. When East takes his ♣A he cannot beat you. If he switches to hearts, you will rise with the ♡A and discard dummy's last heart on the clubs before playing trumps. If instead East plays the ◇K and ◇Q, you will ruff with the ♠9 and lead the ♠Q to East's ♠A. You can ruff his next diamond high too, and draw West's remaining trump. Then you can discard a heart from dummy on your clubs and make the contract, losing only a trump, a diamond and a club.

There was no reason for West to lead a heart but, as it happens, this would have beaten the contract.

PLAY DEAL 11-2

N-S Vul. Dealer West

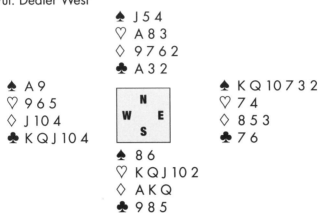

```
                    ♠ J 5 4
                    ♡ A 8 3
                    ◇ 9 7 6 2
                    ♣ A 3 2
  ♠ A 9                            ♠ K Q 10 7 3 2
  ♡ 9 6 5         N                ♡ 7 4
  ◇ J 10 4     W     E             ◇ 8 5 3
  ♣ K Q J 10 4    S                ♣ 7 6
                    ♠ 8 6
                    ♡ K Q J 10 2
                    ◇ A K Q
                    ♣ 9 8 5
```

West	North	East	South
1♣	pass	1♠	2♡
pass	2♠	pass	4♡
all pass			

The Bidding: North, with two great aces, is just worth a cuebid raise of partner's vulnerable two-level overcall. South then decides to bid 4♡.

The Play: West leads the ♣K from his sequence of honors. Take the South cards now. How would you play the heart game?

You start with two potential losers in each black suit. The only realistic chance of reducing the number of losers from four to three is to find a 3-3 diamond break and to discard a spade or a club on the fourth round of diamonds. How will you manage the play?

The diamond suit is blocked. You will need to play the ◇AKQ and then cross to dummy to play the thirteenth diamond. What is your entry to reach dummy's last diamond? The third round of trumps!

You win the club lead with the ace and draw two rounds of trumps with the king and queen. You must then play the three diamond honors. If one of them is ruffed, you could never have made the contract anyway. Today you are lucky and both defenders follow all the way. You return to dummy with the ♡A and discard a loser on the established ◇9. The game is yours.

PLAY DEAL 11-3

Both Vul. Dealer East

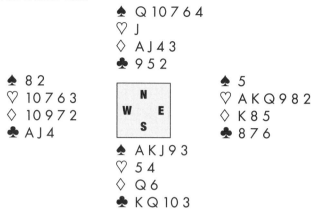

	♠ Q 10 7 6 4	
	♡ J	
	◇ A J 4 3	
	♣ 9 5 2	
♠ 8 2		♠ 5
♡ 10 7 6 3		♡ A K Q 9 8 2
◇ 10 9 7 2		◇ K 8 5
♣ A J 4		♣ 8 7 6
	♠ A K J 9 3	
	♡ 5 4	
	◇ Q 6	
	♣ K Q 10 3	

West	North	East	South
		1♡	1♠
2♡	3♡	pass	4♠
all pass			

The Bidding: North has a great hand in support of spades. Some players might go all the way to 4♠, liking their five-card support. Here North decides to show a 'sound raise to the three-level' with a bid in the opponents' suit. South is happy to accept with his extra values.

The Play: West leads the ♡3 against your contract of 4♠. East wins with the queen and returns the ♣8. You play the ♣K and West wins with the ♣A. How will you continue the play when West switches to a trump?

Once West shows up with the ♣A (also the ♣J, no doubt), East surely holds the ◇K as part of his opening bid. After drawing trumps, you should lead a low diamond from dummy towards your queen. If East rises with the ◇K, you will have two club discards on the diamond suit. If instead East plays low, you will not lose a diamond trick. You will make the game either way.

Did you spot a clever way in which the defenders might have beaten you? When you played your ♣K, West should have ducked and followed with the ♣4. He knows from his partner's ♣8 lead that you hold the ♣KQ10. When East gains the lead subsequently with the ◇K he can then lead a second round of clubs. West will score the ♣A and ♣J and the game will be one down.

PLAY DEAL 11-4

Both Vul. Dealer North

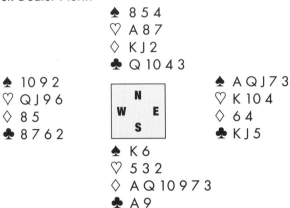

♠ 8 5 4
♡ A 8 7
◇ K J 2
♣ Q 10 4 3

♠ 10 9 2
♡ Q J 9 6
◇ 8 5
♣ 8 7 6 2

♠ A Q J 7 3
♡ K 10 4
◇ 6 4
♣ K J 5

♠ K 6
♡ 5 3 2
◇ A Q 10 9 7 3
♣ A 9

West	North	East	South
	pass	1♠	2◇
pass	2♠	pass	3NT
all pass			

The Bidding: When North hears a vulnerable 2◇ overcall from his partner, his thoughts turn to 3NT. His ◇KJ are likely to solidify partner's suit and he has a precious ace to add to the pile. He cuebids 2♠ to show a sound raise to (at least) the three-level. After this start South expects to score six diamonds, the ♠K and the ♣A. He will then need just one more quick trick from the dummy. His 3NT bid ends the auction.

The Play: West will probably lead the ♠10, which will give you a ninth trick straight away. Suppose he were to lead the ♡Q instead. You would hold up the ♡A for one round, win the second round of hearts and lead a spade towards the king. If East had another heart to play when he took his ♠A (as in the diagram), the suit would be breaking 4-3 and you would make the contract for the loss of one spade and three hearts.

Your hold-up play in hearts would save the contract when West held five hearts to East's two.

BALANCING

It is important not to surrender the auction too soon when the points are fairly evenly divided between the two sides. When you are in the passout seat (the previous two players have passed), you must think carefully whether you should keep the auction open with some bid or a takeout double. Even if your own hand is not too special you may place your partner with a fair hand, simply because the opponents have stopped low. Look at this auction:

LHO	Partner	RHO	You
1♡	pass	pass	?

It sounds as if your side has around half the points in the pack, at least. Your partner may have some 12-14 point hand without the right shape for a bid or a double. In general, you should stretch to keep the bidding open. You should do so even when you would be around a king short of taking action in the direct seat. Suppose you have one of these hands:

(1) ♠ A J 8 7 3
    ♡ 10 5
    ◇ K 10 4 2
    ♣ 8 6

(2) ♠ K 10 7 6
    ♡ 8 6
    ◇ K 8 3
    ♣ K 9 6 5

(3) ♠ A 4 3
    ♡ A J 9
    ◇ 10 8 6 4
    ♣ K 6 2

You should bid 1♠ on (1), double on (2) and bid 1NT on (3). Aware that you may be up to 3 points light for any action in the passout seat, your partner will underbid somewhat with any response.

This is another type of auction where you should be reluctant to pass:

LHO	Partner	RHO	You
1♡	pass	2♡	pass
pass	?		

The opponents have found a heart fit yet made no attempt to reach game. They will surely hold no more than 23 points between them and maybe as few as 18 points. You should freely 'protect' (as it is called) with a takeout double, an unusual 2NT, or a bid in a suit. Even if your own hand is quite weak, you will find your partner with a fair number of points.

PLAY DEAL 12-1

E-W Vul. Dealer West

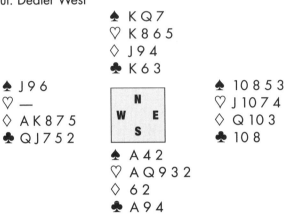

♠ K Q 7
♡ K 8 6 5
◇ J 9 4
♣ K 6 3

♠ J 9 6
♡ —
◇ A K 8 7 5
♣ Q J 7 5 2

♠ 10 8 5 3
♡ J 10 7 4
◇ Q 10 3
♣ 10 8

♠ A 4 2
♡ A Q 9 3 2
◇ 6 2
♣ A 9 4

West	North	East	South
1◇	pass	pass	1♡
pass	2◇	pass	3♡
pass	4♡	all pass	

The Bidding: North has no good bid to make over West's 1◇. He passes and so does East. South, who might have balanced with 1♡ on a much weaker hand than he actually holds, is happy to bid 1♡. North cuebids 2◇ to show a sound raise (see Chapter 11). Realizing that he has strength to spare, South rebids 3♡ instead of just 2♡. This is enough to persuade North to advance to 4♡.

The Play: How would you play 4♡ when West leads ace, king and another diamond to East's queen? You ruff in your hand and see that you have three losers in the side suits — two diamonds and one club. The game will therefore be yours if you can avoid a trump loser. All will be easy if the trump suit breaks no worse than 3-1. There is nothing that you can do if West holds all four trumps. You can pick up ♡J1074 with East, though, as long as you play the ♡K (rather than the ♡A or ♡Q) on the first round.

When you lead a low trump to dummy's king, West shows out. You continue with a second round of trumps from dummy and East inserts the ♡10. You win with the ♡Q, return to dummy with a spade and lead another trump, finessing the ♡9. After drawing East's last trump with the ace, you can claim the contract.

PLAY DEAL 12-2

N-S Vul. Dealer West

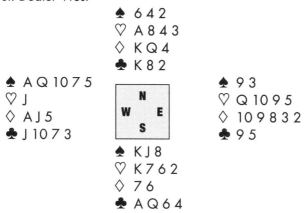

        ♠ 6 4 2
        ♡ A 8 4 3
        ◊ K Q 4
        ♣ K 8 2

♠ A Q 10 7 5   ♠ 9 3
♡ J   ♡ Q 10 9 5
◊ A J 5   ◊ 10 9 8 3 2
♣ J 10 7 3   ♣ 9 5

        ♠ K J 8
        ♡ K 7 6 2
        ◊ 7 6
        ♣ A Q 6 4

West	North	East	South
1♠	pass	pass	1NT
pass	2NT	pass	3NT
all pass			

The Bidding: West's 1♠ is followed by two passes. South would not be strong enough for a 1NT overcall in the second (direct) seat. In the fourth (balancing) seat he is allowed to overbid by up to 3 points. He bids 1NT and North tries for game by raising to 2NT. (He is not inclined to bid a Stayman 2♣ with 3-4-3-3 shape.) South is in the upper part of the 11-14 HCP range and goes to 3NT.

The Play: West leads the ♠7 and South wins East's ♠9 with the ♠J. He can count six top tricks after the spade lead, with a likely two more to come in diamonds. At Trick 2, he plays a diamond to the queen, winning the trick. Where can he find a ninth trick? If West holds three hearts, three rounds of that suit will leave West (the safe hand, who cannot continue spades effectively) on lead. Another chance is that clubs will break 3-3.

Declarer plays the ace and king of hearts and West discards the ◊J. It is beginning to look as if West began with 5-1-3-4 shape. Declarer leads a second round of diamonds towards dummy and West wins with the ace. Unable to play a spade, he exits with the ♣3 to the ♣9 and ♣A. Declarer looks for a 3-3 club break but East shows out on the third round. South's last three cards are the ♠K8 and ♣6. West is thrown on lead with a club and has to give declarer a ninth trick with the ♠K.

PLAY DEAL 12-3

N-S Vul. Dealer West

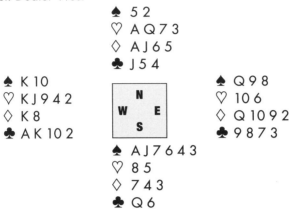

```
                    ♠ 5 2
                    ♡ A Q 7 3
                    ◇ A J 6 5
                    ♣ J 5 4
    ♠ K 10                         ♠ Q 9 8
    ♡ K J 9 4 2         N          ♡ 10 6
    ◇ K 8          W        E      ◇ Q 10 9 2
    ♣ A K 10 2         S          ♣ 9 8 7 3
                    ♠ A J 7 6 4 3
                    ♡ 8 5
                    ◇ 7 4 3
                    ♣ Q 6
```

West	North	East	South
1♡	pass	pass	1♠
pass	1NT	pass	2♠
all pass			

The Bidding: When 1♡ runs to South, he is reluctant to sell out. (West would have made an easy overtrick.) South balances with 1♠. What should North bid now? Because his partner may be up to a king light for a bid in the fourth seat, North should respond just 1NT. South prefers to play in spades with a six-card suit and his correction to 2♠ becomes the final contract.

The Play: West leads the ♣A, his partner playing a discouraging ♣3. If West plays his other top club, he will set up a diamond discard on dummy's ♣J. Appreciating this risk, he switches to the ◇K. This is not really a risky play, since his king will be dead anyway if South holds the ◇Q. In any case, West can see that two diamond tricks will be needed to beat the contract.

Take over the South cards now. How will you play the contract after this start? If you win the first round of diamonds, you will lose two spades, two diamonds and two clubs. A better idea is to hold up the ◇A on the first round. East encourages a diamond continuation and West then plays the ◇8. You win with dummy's ◇A and lead to the ♣Q to set up a club trick. Thanks to your hold-up in diamonds, West now has no diamond to play. You win his club return with the jack, discarding a diamond, and play ace and another trump. An eventual finesse of the ♡Q will give you the contract.

PLAY DEAL 12-4

N-S Vul. Dealer West

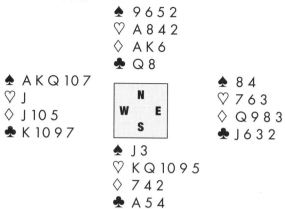

```
                    ♠ 9 6 5 2
                    ♡ A 8 4 2
                    ◇ A K 6
                    ♣ Q 8
♠ A K Q 10 7                        ♠ 8 4
♡ J               N                 ♡ 7 6 3
◇ J 10 5      W       E             ◇ Q 9 8 3
♣ K 10 9 7        S                 ♣ J 6 3 2
                    ♠ J 3
                    ♡ K Q 10 9 5
                    ◇ 7 4 2
                    ♣ A 5 4
```

West	North	East	South
1♠	pass	pass	2♡
pass	4♡	all pass	

The Bidding: South would not be strong enough to overcall 2♡ in the second seat. When 1♠ runs to him in the fourth seat, he expects his partner to hold quite a few points and decides to balance. With his four-card fit, North can visualize a possible game even if South is fairly weak. He goes all the way to 4♡.

The Play: How will you play 4♡ when West cashes two top spades and switches to the ◇J?

You have lost two tricks already and there are two potential further losers in the minor suits. You should plan to lead towards the ♣Q, establishing a discard for dummy's losing diamond. You win the diamond switch and draw trumps with the ace, king and queen. You then lead a club towards dummy, hoping that West holds the ♣K. He rises with that card and plays another diamond. You win in the dummy, cash the ♣Q and return to your hand with a spade ruff. You then discard dummy's last diamond on the ♣A and ruff a diamond in dummy. The contract is yours.

13

HELP-SUIT GAME TRIES

You open 1♡ or 1♠ and partner raises you to the two-level. When you have a hand in the middle range, around 15-17 points, game may depend on a good fit between the hands. By using help-suit game tries, telling partner the suit where you have some losers to cover, you can give yourself the best chance of reaching the right final contract.

You		You	Partner
♠ K Q J		1♡	2♡
♡ A Q J 9 3		3♣	
◇ 8			
♣ Q 6 5 3			

You are uncertain whether to bid 4♡ and decide to make a game try. Your 3♣ bid passes this message (hearts are already agreed as trumps). It shows a suit of at least three cards, one containing at least two losers.

If partner has:

♠ 9 7 2 ♡ K 8 7 4 ◇ 10 7 2 ♣ K J 7

he will bid 4♡. His ♣KJ7 is a useful holding in the help-suit. It will reduce the number of losers there. A singleton or doubleton in the help-suit would also be a great holding, allowing you to ruff one or more of your losers in the dummy. If instead partner held:

♠ 9 7 2 ♡ K 8 7 4 ◇ K J 7 ♣ 10 7 2

he would sign off in 3♡. Three low cards is just about the least helpful holding possible! Indeed, you would need some luck to make even 3♡.

While you should look closely at your holding in the help-suit, it would not be a sensible to ignore the rest of your hand. Holding four trumps rather than three is always worth a bit. Holding 9 points rather than 6 is also an advantage. So, when your fit in the help-suit is neither very good, nor very bad, look at the general strength of your hand.

1♠ – 2♠ – 2NT is also a game try, showing around 17-18 points and no particularly weak suit. Responder would tend to raise to game with 8-9 points and bid only 3♠ with 6-7 points.

PLAY DEAL 13-1

Neither Vul. Dealer South

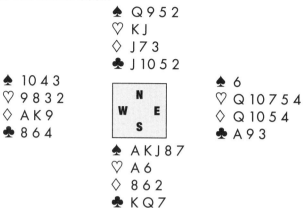

♠ Q 9 5 2
♡ K J
◇ J 7 3
♣ J 10 5 2

♠ 10 4 3
♡ 9 8 3 2
◇ A K 9
♣ 8 6 4

♠ 6
♡ Q 10 7 5 4
◇ Q 10 5 4
♣ A 9 3

♠ A K J 8 7
♡ A 6
◇ 8 6 2
♣ K Q 7

West	North	East	South
			1♠
pass	2♠	pass	3◇
pass	3♠	all pass	

The Bidding: South sees a chance of game when partner raises to 2♠. Game prospects may depend on whether North can provide any help in the diamond suit, where South holds several losers. He therefore makes a help-suit game try of 3◇. How should North respond?

North holds 8 HCP, a reasonable number for his raise, but he has absolutely no help at all in diamonds. (An honor or two in the suit would have been helpful, as would a shortage that would allow South to ruff a diamond or two.) North signs off in 3♠ and the partnership stops safely short of game, despite holding 25 HCP between them.

The Play: There is nothing much to the play. The defenders begin by cashing three rounds of diamonds. They score the ♣A subsequently but declarer is able to claim the remainder. That's +140 to North-South, the reward for diagnosing that their two hands did not fit well together.

N-S Vul. Dealer South

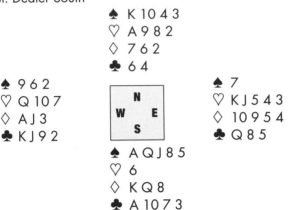

```
                    ♠ K 10 4 3
                    ♡ A 9 8 2
                    ◇ 7 6 2
                    ♣ 6 4
    ♠ 9 6 2                           ♠ 7
    ♡ Q 10 7          N               ♡ K J 5 4 3
    ◇ A J 3       W       E           ◇ 10 9 5 4
    ♣ K J 9 2         S               ♣ Q 8 5
                    ♠ A Q J 8 5
                    ♡ 6
                    ◇ K Q 8
                    ♣ A 10 7 3
```

West	North	East	South
			1♠
pass	2♠	pass	3♣
pass	4♠	all pass	

The Bidding: South judges that it would be an overbid to raise directly to 4♠. He decides to make a help-suit game try. To allow his partner to judge the matter accurately, he bids 3♣ to show that he has losers to be covered in that suit. North holds only 7 HCP but he has shortage in the help-suit (clubs), which will allow his partner to score a ruff or two there. He also holds four trumps rather than three, always a promising sign. He bids 4♠, concluding the auction.

The Play: West holds good cards in the help-suit. He leads a low trump with the aim of reducing the number of club ruffs in the dummy. Declarer wins with the ♠8. Should he draw a second round of trumps now? No, because he will have to surrender a club trick before he can score any ruffs in that suit and the defenders might then be able to draw a third round of trumps.

Declarer continues with ace and another club instead, preparing for his club ruffs. West wins the second round and plays another trump, East showing out. Nothing can stop declarer from ruffing two clubs in the dummy, using a heart ruff as the entry for the second ruff. He then plays a diamond and is soon able to reach his hand to draw West's last trump. Declarer loses just two diamonds and one club.

PLAY DEAL 13-3

Both Vul. Dealer South

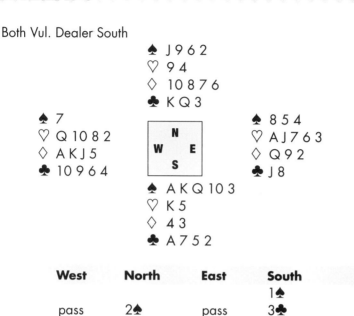

♠ J 9 6 2
♡ 9 4
◇ 10 8 7 6
♣ K Q 3

♠ 7
♡ Q 10 8 2
◇ A K J 5
♣ 10 9 6 4

♠ 8 5 4
♡ A J 7 6 3
◇ Q 9 2
♣ J 8

♠ A K Q 10 3
♡ K 5
◇ 4 3
♣ A 7 5 2

West	North	East	South
			1♠
pass	2♠	pass	3♣
pass	4♠	all pass	

The Bidding: South can see a chance of game if partner can help him with his losers in the club suit. North does not have much of a hand for his raise to 2♠, but there are two positive features. Firstly, he holds four trumps instead of three, always a good sign. Secondly, he has the king and queen of partner's help suit. It is often worth stretching to bid a vulnerable game and he does indeed leap to 4♠.

The Play: How will you play the spade game when West leads the ◇A, ◇K and ◇5 to East's ◇Q?

You ruff the third round of diamonds and draw trumps in three rounds. If clubs break 3-3, you will be able to discard a heart from dummy on the thirteenth club. You can then ruff a heart in dummy for your tenth trick. When you test the clubs, an even break does not materialize. You return to dummy by ruffing your last club… take a deep breath and… lead a heart towards the king. East holds the ♡A, so you make the contract.

Yes, you might well have gone down if West held the ♡A. The 500 bonus for making a vulnerable game means that it is well worth bidding games that are a 50% chance, even those that are slightly worse than that.

PLAY DEAL 13-4

N-S Vul. Dealer North

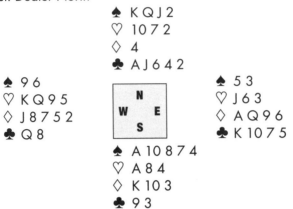

```
                      ♠ K Q J 2
                      ♡ 10 7 2
                      ◇ 4
                      ♣ A J 6 4 2
  ♠ 9 6                              ♠ 5 3
  ♡ K Q 9 5          N               ♡ J 6 3
  ◇ J 8 7 5 2    W       E           ◇ A Q 9 6
  ♣ Q 8              S               ♣ K 10 7 5
                      ♠ A 10 8 7 4
                      ♡ A 8 4
                      ◇ K 10 3
                      ♣ 9 3
```

West	North	East	South
	1♣	pass	1♠
pass	2♠	pass	3♡
pass	3♠	all pass	

The Bidding: North has a minimum opening bid and raises partner's spades to the two-level. South reckons that he has game try values. Since a heart shortage opposite the ace would be welcome, he decides to make a game try of 3♡ rather than 3◇. North has a very unhelpful heart holding and signs off in 3♠, ending the auction.

The Play: Look at the West hand. What would you lead against a contract of either 3♠ or 4♠? It is natural to choose one of the red suits and the two touching honors in hearts make this suit the better choice. West leads the ♡K and declarer cannot then avoid losing two hearts, one diamond and one club.

Take declarer's cards next and imagine that you are in 4♠, with West leading a trump (not the best lead). How will you play? You need to discard one of your heart losers. One chance is to develop the clubs, hoping for a 3-3 break. Another is to lead towards the ◇K, hoping that East holds the ace.

If you duck a club, the defenders will surely switch to hearts. You will then lose the chance of finding the ◇A onside; you will have to rely on a 3-3 club break with only a 36% chance. It is better to lead a diamond towards the king, taking the 50% chance that East holds the ◇A. Here, that chance would pay off. You would be able to discard a heart from dummy on the ◇K and ruff a heart for your tenth trick.

14

CONTROL-SHOWING CUEBIDS

You open 1♠ and your partner raises to 3♠. Suppose you bid 4◊ next, what can that mean? Since you are committed to game, at least, the purpose of 4◊ must be to show a strong hand and to suggest a slam. When you play control-showing cuebids, 4◊ will show a first-round diamond control (the ◊A or a void in diamonds). Since you always show your cheapest first-round control in a side suit, your 4◊ will deny the ♣A (or a club void).

When a trump suit has been agreed, a bid in a new suit at the four-level or higher is a control-showing cuebid. When hearts have been agreed, 3♠ is also a control-showing cuebid.

You	You	Partner
♠ A 9 5 4		1♠
♡ A 10 7 6 2	3♠	4♣
◊ Q 5	4♡	4♠
♣ 8 6		

Partner suggests a slam with his 4♣, showing a first-round club control. You reciprocate by making a cuebid too: 4♡, which denies a first-round control in diamonds. Partner thinks he has done his hand justice by making one slam try and signs off in 4♠.

It is possible that partner holds the ◊K. However, with that card and a very strong hand overall, he had the option of cuebidding 5◊ on the third round (showing a second-round control). You should pass now.

There are two main purposes in a control-showing cuebid:

· to tell partner that you are interested in a slam
· to detect whether you have a side suit where the defenders can cash the ace and king right away

For a slam to be possible, you will need first-round control of three suits and at least second-round control of the fourth suit. You should not use Blackwood when you have two or three small cards in a suit, or when you have a void. That is the time to use a cuebid.

PLAY DEAL 14-1

Neither Vul. Dealer South.

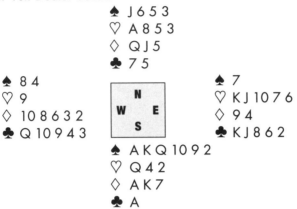

♠ J 6 5 3
♡ A 8 5 3
◇ Q J 5
♣ 7 5

♠ 8 4
♡ 9
◇ 10 8 6 3 2
♣ Q 10 9 4 3

♠ 7
♡ K J 10 7 6
◇ 9 4
♣ K J 8 6 2

♠ A K Q 10 9 2
♡ Q 4 2
◇ A K 7
♣ A

West	North	East	South
			2♣
pass	2◇	pass	2♠
pass	3♠	pass	4♣
pass	4♡	pass	6♠
all pass			

The Bidding: South shows his power by opening with a strong 2♣. North responds 2◇, since he has no particularly strong suit to show with a positive response. When South rebids 2♠, North raises to 3♠ to set the trump suit. South can see the possibility of a slam and cuebids 4♣. North then cuebids 4♡ to show a heart control and South leaps to 6♠.

The Play: One of the best opening leads against a suit contract is a side-suit singleton and West is happy to lead the ♡9. How should you then play the contract?

It may be tempting to play a low card from dummy, running the lead to your ♡Q to set up a second heart winner. Look what will happen! East will win with the ♡K and give his partner a heart ruff, beating the slam.

It is obvious from the opening lead that East holds the ♡K. You should win the first trick with the ♡A and draw trumps with the ♠A and ♣J. You can then lead towards the ♡Q to set up your twelfth trick.

PLAY DEAL 14-2

Both Vul. Dealer South.

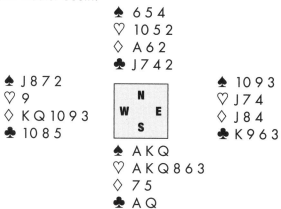

```
                    ♠ 6 5 4
                    ♡ 10 5 2
                    ◇ A 6 2
                    ♣ J 7 4 2
   ♠ J 8 7 2                      ♠ 10 9 3
   ♡ 9              N             ♡ J 7 4
   ◇ K Q 10 9 3   W   E           ◇ J 8 4
   ♣ 10 8 5          S            ♣ K 9 6 3
                    ♠ A K Q
                    ♡ A K Q 8 6 3
                    ◇ 7 5
                    ♣ A Q
```

West	North	East	South
			2♣
pass	2◇	pass	2♡
pass	3♡	pass	3♠
pass	4◇	pass	6♡
all pass			

The Bidding: Once again, South shows a powerful hand by opening with a strong 2♣. North responds 2◇ and South rebids 2♡ (game-forcing). When North raises to 3♡, setting the trump suit, South can see the possibility of a slam and cuebids 3♠. North then cuebids 4◇ to show the ◇A. Willing to venture a slam now, South bids 6♡.

The Play: How will you play 6♡ when West leads the ◇K?

You win with dummy's ◇A and see that after this opening lead you will need the club finesse to be right to make the slam. (After a less effective major-suit lead, you would have been able to draw trumps and play the ♣A and ♣Q to set up a diamond discard on the ♣J.) Should you draw trumps after winning the first trick? No, because unless the ♡J falls in two rounds you will have no entry back to dummy to take a club finesse later.

You must hope for the best and finesse the ♣Q at Trick 2. Luck is with you on this occasion and the finesse wins! You draw trumps and make the slam, losing just one trick in diamonds.

PLAY DEAL 14-3

Neither Vul. Dealer South.

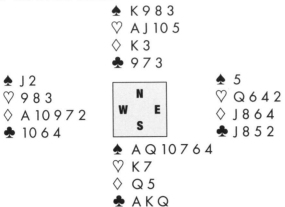

```
                    ♠ K 9 8 3
                    ♡ A J 10 5
                    ◇ K 3
                    ♣ 9 7 3
    ♠ J 2                             ♠ 5
    ♡ 9 8 3          N               ♡ Q 6 4 2
    ◇ A 10 9 7 2   W   E             ◇ J 8 6 4
    ♣ 10 6 4         S               ♣ J 8 5 2
                    ♠ A Q 10 7 6 4
                    ♡ K 7
                    ◇ Q 5
                    ♣ A K Q
```

West	North	East	South
			1♠
pass	3♠	pass	4♣
pass	4♡	pass	5♣
pass	5◇	pass	6♠
all pass			

The Bidding: When South hears a double raise in spades, he can envisage a slam. He cuebids 4♣ and partner then cuebids 4♡. What does this mean? It tells South two things: that North holds first-round control of hearts, also that he does not hold first-round control of diamonds.

Can South now rule out a slam? No, because North might still hold the ◇K. South continues with a second cuebid in clubs, showing the ♣K. North can now show his second-round control in diamonds. Pleased with the news that he has just heard, South leaps to 6♠. If North had instead bid 5♠ at his second turn, this would deny the ◇K and South would pass. He would know that the defenders could cash the first two tricks in diamonds.

'How does South know that North held the ♠K?' you may be thinking. It's a good question and the answer is that he cannot be certain of that. North probably holds the ♠K. If he doesn't, then a trump finesse may be necessary.

It's worth bidding a slam that is probably cold but may require a finesse.

The Play: Once you have managed the bidding correctly, you deserve to be rewarded occasionally with absolutely no problem in the play! This is one such deal.

PLAY DEAL 14-4

Neither Vul. Dealer South.

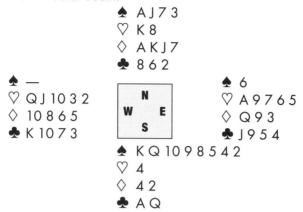

```
                    ♠ A J 7 3
                    ♡ K 8
                    ♢ A K J 7
                    ♣ 8 6 2
♠ —                                    ♠ 6
♡ Q J 10 3 2          N               ♡ A 9 7 6 5
♢ 10 8 6 5        W       E           ♢ Q 9 3
♣ K 10 7 3            S               ♣ J 9 5 4
                    ♠ K Q 10 9 8 5 4 2
                    ♡ 4
                    ♢ 4 2
                    ♣ A Q
```

West	North	East	South
			1♠
pass	2NT	pass	3♡
pass	4♢	pass	4NT
pass	5♡	pass	6♠
all pass			

The Bidding: North shows a strong spade raise with his Jacoby 2NT (see Chapter 9). South's 3♡ shows a singleton heart. Although North realizes that his ♡K may now have limited value, he is happy to cuebid in diamonds. South has the clubs controlled as well as holding eight magnificent trumps. He bids Blackwood (or Roman Keycard Blackwood), leaping to 6♠ when he hears that partner has two aces.

The Play: How will you play the slam when West leads the ♡Q? With only two hearts in dummy, you might as well try the ♡K. It loses to the ♡A, of course, and you ruff the heart return. What now?

A successful finesse in either diamonds or clubs will give you a twelfth trick. If your chosen finesse loses, though, you will be one down whether or not the other finesse was onside. On such deals you must aim to combine two chances rather than rely on just one. After drawing trumps, play the ♢AK and ruff a diamond in your hand. As it happens, the ♢Q falls and you will have a diamond discard for your ♣Q. If your first chance (dropping the ♢Q) fails, you will fall back on a second chance, finessing the ♣Q.

15

THE GRAND SLAM FORCE

The Grand Slam Force (GSF) is a specialized 5NT bid used during slam auctions. It asks: 'Do you hold two of the three top trump honors?' If so, you jump to a grand slam. Otherwise you bid six of the agreed trump suit.

Partner	You
	2♣
2♦	2♠
3♠	5NT

♠ A J 9 8 6   ♡ A K   ♢ A K Q J 4   ♣ A

Once you find a spade fit, you can see that a grand slam will be the right contract when partner's trumps include the king and queen. If partner holds those two honors, he bids 7♠ now. Otherwise he signs off in 6♠.

Note that Roman Keycard Blackwood (see Chapter 20) also allows you to investigate which of the three top trump honors your partner holds. On this particular deal, you could have used that method instead.

In the auction above, spades were explicitly agreed. Suppose the bidding starts 3♢ – 5NT instead. The 5NT bid agrees diamonds as trumps and asks the opener to bid 6♢ or 7♢, depending on whether he holds two of the top three diamond honors. The same would be true on this bidding: 1♠ – 2♦ – 2♡ – 5NT. Responder's 5NT agrees hearts as trumps and asks partner to bid 7♡ if he holds two of the three top trump honors.

Except when clubs are trumps, there is space for three or more responses. After 1♢ – 3♢ – 5NT, for example, you would respond:

6♣	1 of the top three trump honors
6♢	0 of the top three (a sign-off is the weakest option)
7♢	2 of the top three.

There are two particular situations where 5NT is not a grand slam force. The first is when you have already bid a Blackwood 4NT. In that case a 5NT follow-up usually asks partner how many kings he holds. The other exception is when you raise 1NT or 2NT to 5NT. You are then asking partner to judge whether the final contract should be 6NT or 7NT.

PLAY DEAL 15-1

N-S Vul. Dealer South.

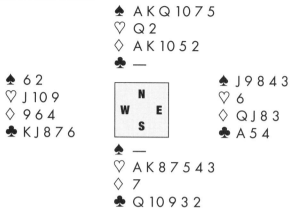

```
                    ♠ A K Q 10 7 5
                    ♡ Q 2
                    ◇ A K 10 5 2
                    ♣ —
  ♠ 6 2                              ♠ J 9 8 4 3
  ♡ J 10 9          N                ♡ 6
  ◇ 9 6 4       W       E            ◇ Q J 8 3
  ♣ K J 8 7 6       S                ♣ A 5 4
                    ♠ —
                    ♡ A K 8 7 5 4 3
                    ◇ 7
                    ♣ Q 10 9 3 2
```

West	North	East	South
			4♡
pass	5NT	pass	7♡
all pass			

The Bidding: South opens with a high bid, to make it difficult for the opponents to find a profitable contract in one of his short suits. North decides that he wants partner to play in 7♡ if he holds the ♡AK.

The Play: West leads the ♡J against the grand slam. How would you play the contract?

The first trick will confirm that trumps are not 4-0. You will then be able to count seven heart tricks and five top winners in the dummy, for a total of twelve. Suppose you win the trump lead with the ♡Q, ruff a spade in your hand and draw the remaining trumps. If spades break 4-3 (or the ♠J is doubleton), you will be able to discard all five of your club losers. As the cards lie, with East holding five spades, you will go one down.

Rather than rely on a good spade break, you should aim to ruff one club in dummy for your thirteenth trick. You win with the ♡Q (saving the ♡2 for the club ruff) and reach your hand with a spade ruff. You ruff a club with the ♡2 and return to your hand with a second spade ruff. You can then draw trumps and cross to the ◇A to discard your remaining clubs on dummy's winning honor cards.

E-W Vul. Dealer North.

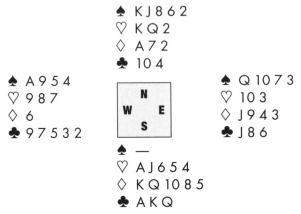

♠ K J 8 6 2
♡ K Q 2
◇ A 7 2
♣ 10 4

♠ A 9 5 4
♡ 9 8 7
◇ 6
♣ 9 7 5 3 2

♠ Q 10 7 3
♡ 10 3
◇ J 9 4 3
♣ J 8 6

♠ —
♡ A J 6 5 4
◇ K Q 10 8 5
♣ A K Q

West	North	East	South
	1♠	pass	2♡
pass	3♡	pass	4♣
pass	4◇	pass	5NT
pass	7♡	all pass	

The Bidding: When hearts are agreed as trumps, South cuebids his ♣A. He receives good news when North cuebids the ◇A. South now fancies a grand slam, provided North holds the king and queen of trumps. He bids 5NT and North duly leaps to 7♡.

The Play: How would you play 7♡ when West leads the ♡9? (Note that it would be a poor idea for him to lead the ♠A. For South's 5NT to make any sense, he must be void in spades.)

You win the trump lead and draw trumps in two more rounds. All now depends on picking up the diamond suit for no loser. You should play the ◇K on the first round and then cross to the ◇A. When West shows out on the second round, you know that it is necessary to finesse the ◇10. After taking this 'marked finesse' (as it is called) you draw East's last diamond with the ◇Q and claim the remaining tricks.

Suppose you had played the ◇A on the first round. You would have no reason to finesse the ◇10 on the next round. When you played a diamond to the king, West would show out. With no way to return to the dummy, you would be one down.

PLAY DEAL 15-3

N-S Vul. Dealer North.

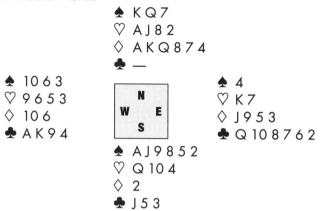

♠ K Q 7
♡ A J 8 2
◇ A K Q 8 7 4
♣ —

♠ 10 6 3
♡ 9 6 5 3
◇ 10 6
♣ A K 9 4

♠ 4
♡ K 7
◇ J 9 5 3
♣ Q 10 8 7 6 2

♠ A J 9 8 5 2
♡ Q 10 4
◇ 2
♣ J 5 3

West	North	East	South
	1◇	pass	1♠
pass	2♡	pass	2♠
pass	5NT	pass	6♣
pass	7♠	all pass	

The Bidding: North's reverse to 2♡ is forcing and South rebids his spades. North is now willing to play in 7♠ if South holds the ♠A. Blackwood would not be of much use because if South showed one ace it might be the ♣A. North therefore bids 5NT, asking partner how many of the three top trump honors he holds. A 6♠ response (the sign-off is the weakest option) would show none of the top three; 7♠ would show two of the top three. South's response of 6♣ shows one honor, which must be the ace, and the grand slam is duly reached.

The Play: How would you play 7♠ when West leads the ♣A?

You ruff with dummy's ♠7 and play the ♠KQ, East showing out on the second round. If diamonds are no worse than 4-2, you can set up the suit and discard two clubs and two hearts, not needing the heart finesse. You play the ◇A and ruff a diamond with the ♠J, pleased to see West follow suit. You draw the last trump with your ♠A and return to dummy with the ♡A to throw your four remaining losers on the established ◇KQ87.

If West had shown out on the second round of diamonds, you would have had to draw his last trump and rely on a finesse against the ♡K.

Both Vul. Dealer North.

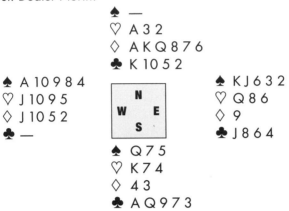

```
                    ♠ —
                    ♡ A 3 2
                    ◇ A K Q 8 7 6
                    ♣ K 10 5 2
♠ A 10 9 8 4                        ♠ K J 6 3 2
♡ J 10 9 5          N              ♡ Q 8 6
◇ J 10 5 2      W       E          ◇ 9
♣ —                 S              ♣ J 8 6 4
                    ♠ Q 7 5
                    ♡ K 7 4
                    ◇ 4 3
                    ♣ A Q 9 7 3
```

West	North	East	South
	1◇	pass	2♣
pass	5NT	pass	7♣
all pass			

The Bidding: When North hears a response in clubs, he can visualize a grand slam if South holds the ♣A and ♣Q. He bids 5NT, a grand slam force, to discover if partner does hold two of the three top honors. South duly rebids 7♣, bringing the auction to a close.

The Play: West leads the ♡J against the grand slam. How would you play the contract?

It is essential to win with the ♡K, retaining the ♡A as a later entry to dummy. You play the ♣A next (so that you can pick up ♣J864 in either defender's hand). West shows out and the time has come to ruff a spade. You ruff the ♠5 with dummy's ♣10. This allows you to play the ♣K and lead the carefully preserved ♣5 for a finesse of the ♣9 in your hand. You then draw East's last trump with the ♣Q, discarding dummy's ♡2.

You play the ◇AK, discovering a 4-1 break. That's no problem! You ruff a diamond with your last trump and reenter dummy with the ♡A to score the remaining tricks with the ◇Q87.

MICHAELS CUEBIDS AND UNUSUAL NT

A Michaels cuebid is a bid in the suit that an opponent has opened. A minor-suit Michaels bid shows both majors. A major-suit Michaels bid shows the other major and an unspecified minor. The shape will be at least 5-5.

♠ Q J 9 8 5
♡ K Q 10 6 4
◇ 7
♣ 9 3

LHO	Partner	RHO	You
		1◇	2◇

Your 2◇ Michaels cuebid shows both majors. Many players like 'weak or strong Michaels', making the bid when they hold either 6-10 or 16+ HCP. With the strong type, they intend to bid again over a minimum response. With a hand of 11-15 HCP, they would overcall 1♠ instead.

♠ A K 10 7 2
♡ A 3
◇ 8
♣ K Q 10 7 6

LHO	Partner	RHO	You
		1♡	2♡

Here you are in the strong range. 2♡ shows spades and an unspecified minor. Partner may bid 2NT to ask you to bid your minor. Here you would rebid 4♣ rather than 3♣ to show a strong hand.

When partner has a major-suit fit, he can sign off in that suit at the two-level, make a game try or raise to game. If partner were to bid 2♠ on the hand above, you would raise to 3♠ to show 16+ HCP.

A similar convention is the Unusual Notrump, a 2NT overcall showing at least 5-5 shape in the lowest unbid suits.

♠ 5
♡ 7 6
◇ K Q 10 9 4
♣ A J 8 7 2

LHO	Partner	RHO	You
		1♡/1♠	2NT

If LHO passes, your partner will usually bid three of his better minor. With a good fit or a strong hand, he can make a higher response. A 2NT bid after two passes is natural (showing 20-21 HCP), and not the Unusual Notrump.

E-W Vul. Dealer West.

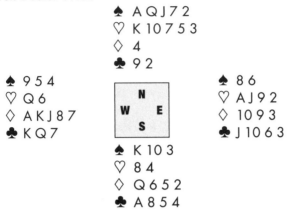

♠ A Q J 7 2
♡ K 10 7 5 3
◇ 4
♣ 9 2

♠ 9 5 4
♡ Q 6
◇ A K J 8 7
♣ K Q 7

♠ 8 6
♡ A J 9 2
◇ 10 9 3
♣ J 10 6 3

♠ K 10 3
♡ 8 4
◇ Q 6 5 2
♣ A 8 5 4

West	North	East	South
1◇	2◇	pass	2♠
all pass			

The Bidding: North bids a Michaels 2◇ to show both majors. South assumes initially that North is in the 'weak' 6-10 HCP range and responds just 2♠. East-West could have done quite well in diamonds but neither player feels able to contest the auction further.

The Play: West cashes the ◇A and switches to a trump. How will you play the contract?

You win with the ♠10 in your hand and should then tackle the heart side suit. There is no need to play a heart to the king immediately; indeed, that would lead to defeat. You should run the ♡8, leaving a possible lead to the king until the second round. East wins with the ♡9 and returns another trump, which you win with the jack. A club to the ace allows you to lead a second round of hearts towards the dummy. When the ♡Q appears, this is covered by the king and ace. East plays a diamond and you ruff in the dummy. You can then draw the last trump and use your ♡107 to force out East's ♡J, establishing dummy's last two hearts. The contract is yours.

PLAY DEAL 16-2

Neither Vul. Dealer West.

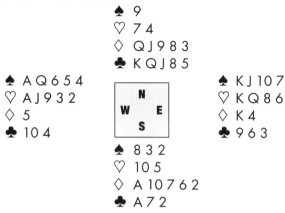

```
                    ♠ 9
                    ♡ 7 4
                    ◇ Q J 9 8 3
                    ♣ K Q J 8 5
  ♠ A Q 6 5 4                      ♠ K J 10 7
  ♡ A J 9 3 2         N            ♡ K Q 8 6
  ◇ 5            W         E       ◇ K 4
  ♣ 10 4              S            ♣ 9 6 3
                    ♠ 8 3 2
                    ♡ 10 5
                    ◇ A 10 7 6 2
                    ♣ A 7 2
```

West	North	East	South
1♠	2NT	4♠	5◇
dbl	all pass		

The Bidding: North bids the Unusual Notrump, showing at least 5-5 shape in the minor suits. East raises to 4♠ and South must decide whether he should sacrifice in 5◇. Since his two aces lie in partner's suits, there is some chance that five tricks can be made in each of the minors, which will be only one down. The five-card fit for partner's diamonds suggests that few defensive diamond tricks will be available against 4♠. South decides to sacrifice in 5◇ and West doubles.

The Play: How would you defend on the West cards? A trump lead would surrender control of the hand and would prove disastrous; declarer would be able to score a doubled overtrick, discarding both his hearts on dummy's clubs. You should lead the ♠A. When dummy goes down, it is clear that no further spade tricks can be taken. Equally clear is the risk that heart tricks might disappear on dummy's clubs. West should therefore switch to the ♡A. East gives an encouraging signal in hearts and a second round of that suit puts the game one down (declarer picking up the trumps with a finesse).

Although the heart switch was fairly obvious on this deal, East should give a suit preference signal when dummy's singleton spade appears. He should play a high spade (the ♠J) to ask partner to switch to the higher of the two remaining side suits (hearts).

PLAY DEAL 16-3

N-S Vul. Dealer West.

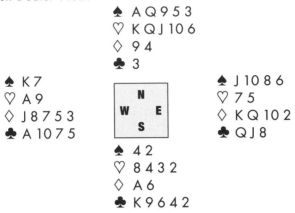

	♠ A Q 9 5 3	
	♡ K Q J 10 6	
	◇ 9 4	
	♣ 3	

♠ K 7   ♠ J 10 8 6
♡ A 9   ♡ 7 5
◇ J 8 7 5 3   ◇ K Q 10 2
♣ A 10 7 5   ♣ Q J 8

	♠ 4 2	
	♡ 8 4 3 2	
	◇ A 6	
	♣ K 9 6 4 2	

West	North	East	South
1◇	2◇	3◇	3♡
pass	4♡	all pass	

The Bidding: North enters with a Michaels cuebid of 2◇. East competes with 3◇ and South is happy to bid 3♡. North has a close decision at his next turn. His hand is good but nothing special. However, he sees that there may be a chance of game if South holds as little as the ♡A and the ♠10. It might then be possible to score five tricks in each major. Not one to turn a blind eye to the chance of a vulnerable game, North raises to 4♡.

The Play: How will you play 4♡ when West leads the ◇5 to East's ◇Q?
    You win with the ◇A and see that you will need to find the ♠K onside to give yourself a chance. Since the spades need to be established, perhaps with a couple of ruffs, it makes good sense to finesse the ♠Q at Trick 2. (This often happens. Although you cannot calculate exactly how the play will go, you sense that you should tackle the main side suit straight away.) The spade finesse wins and you play dummy's ♡K. West wins and crosses to partner's ◇K, East returning the ♣Q. You play low from your hand and ruff the next club in dummy. The ♡Q draws the outstanding trumps and you continue with ace and another spade, ruffing in your hand. The suit breaks 4-2 but you can return to dummy with a club ruff to set up the spades with another ruff in your hand. You lose just a trump, a diamond and a club, making your game.

PLAY DEAL 16-4

Neither Vul. Dealer South.

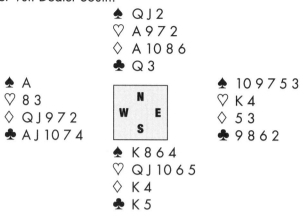

```
                    ♠ Q J 2
                    ♡ A 9 7 2
                    ◇ A 10 8 6
                    ♣ Q 3
    ♠ A                            ♠ 10 9 7 5 3
    ♡ 8 3           N              ♡ K 4
    ◇ Q J 9 7 2   W   E            ◇ 5 3
    ♣ A J 10 7 4    S              ♣ 9 8 6 2
                    ♠ K 8 6 4
                    ♡ Q J 10 6 5
                    ◇ K 4
                    ♣ K 5
```

West	North	East	South
			1♡
2NT	4♡	all pass	

The Bidding: West enters with the Unusual Notrump, showing at least 5-5 shape in the minor suits. With four-card support for hearts and 13 points, North raises to 4♡. Although East holds four-card club support, he expects 5♣ doubled to go at least 300 down. It could cost more than this, so he decides not to sacrifice.

The Play: West leads the ♣A, hoping that he can then reach his partner's hand to receive a spade ruff. With the ◇A on display in the dummy, West's best hope of putting East on lead is that he holds the ♣K. He plays the ♣A and another club, South winning the trick. How should declarer continue?

There are only two losing tricks in the side suits, a spade and a club. Declarer can therefore afford a trump loser. What he cannot afford is to take a losing trump finesse, followed by a spade ruff by West. This would give the defenders a fourth trick and defeat the contract.

To avoid this scenario, declarer plays a trump to the ace followed by a second round of trumps. East wins with the ♡K but the defenders score only three tricks and the game is made.

LANDY 2♣ OVER OPPONENTS' 1NT

Landy is a simple but effective convention to play over an opponent's 1NT opening, whether that is weak or strong. An overcall of 2♣ shows at least 5-4 shape in the major suits and enough strength to play at the two-level. The upper limit is around 15 points because with more than that you would make a penalty double. Here's an example:

You		LHO	Partner	RHO	You
♠ K Q 9 5 2				1NT	2♣
♡ A 10 8 6					
◊ Q 2					
♣ 8 5					

Partner will often respond 2♡ or 2♠, showing his better fit, and you will then pass. If partner has no fit for either major and long clubs, he is allowed to pass 2♣:

You	Partner	LHO	Partner	RHO	You
♠ A 10 7 6	♠ 8 3			1NT	2♣
♡ K J 9 7 6	♡ 10 2	pass	pass		
◊ Q 8 3	◊ K 9 6				
♣ 10	♣ K Q 9 7 5 2				

A response of 2◊ indicates equal length in the majors (often 3-3) and asks the Landy bidder to show his better major.

Occasionally, partner will have a very good fit for one of your suits and can invite a game by bidding 3♡ or 3♠. He may even be strong enough to bid game in one of your suits. The only artificial response is 3♣, which shows a strong hand and asks for more information. For example, you would then rebid 3♡ to show that you had five hearts on the hand above.

Remember that the main purpose of the bid is to contest the partscore. Unless you have a very good fit, it is unlikely that you will want to play at the game-level, particularly against a strong 1NT.

An overcall of 2♣ retains the same meaning (both majors) in the fourth seat, after 1NT – pass – pass.

PLAY DEAL 17-1

E-W Vul. Dealer West

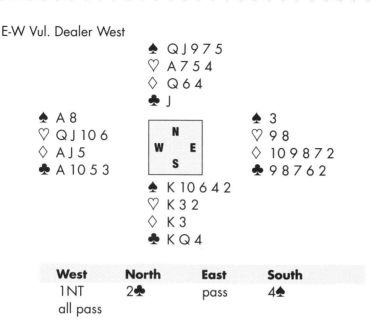

	♠ Q J 9 7 5	
	♡ A 7 5 4	
	◇ Q 6 4	
	♣ J	

♠ A 8
♡ Q J 10 6
◇ A J 5
♣ A 10 5 3

♠ 3
♡ 9 8
◇ 10 9 8 7 2
♣ 9 8 7 6 2

♠ K 10 6 4 2
♡ K 3 2
◇ K 3
♣ K Q 4

West	North	East	South
1NT	2♣	pass	4♠
all pass			

The Bidding: North enters the auction with a Landy 2♣, showing a hand that is at least 5-4 in the majors. With five-card spade support and 14 HCP, South decides to bid game in spades.

The Play: West leads the ♡Q. What is your plan in 4♠?

What will happen if you win the first trick and play a trump? West will win with the ♠A and lead another round of hearts, removing your last stopper in the suit. With no way to avoid a loser in every suit, you will go one down.

What mistake would any declarer have made if he followed that line of play? Right, he would have forgotten to make a plan for the contract. You start with four potential losers in the South hand and must look for a plan to reduce this number to three. You can hardly avoid the defenders scoring their three aces, so you must seek to avoid a heart loser. This can be done by setting up the club suit for discards.

You win the first trick with the ♡A and lead the ♣J. West has to win or you would not lose a club trick. You win the heart continuation with the ♡K and — thanks to winning the first trick in the right hand — you can discard dummy's two remaining hearts on the ♣KQ. It will then be safe to draw trumps and you will make the contract.

PLAY DEAL 17-2

Neither Vul. Dealer East

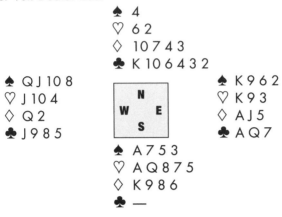

```
                    ♠ 4
                    ♡ 6 2
                    ◊ 10 7 4 3
                    ♣ K 10 6 4 3 2
  ♠ Q J 10 8              ♠ K 9 6 2
  ♡ J 10 4          N     ♡ K 9 3
  ◊ Q 2         W      E  ◊ A J 5
  ♣ J 9 8 5          S     ♣ A Q 7
                    ♠ A 7 5 3
                    ♡ A Q 8 7 5
                    ◊ K 9 8 6
                    ♣ —
```

West	North	East	South
		1NT	2♣
pass	pass	all pass	

The Bidding: South enters the auction with a Landy 2♣, showing a hand that is at least 5-4 in the majors. Worried that South may hold only four hearts, North decides to pass out 2♣.

The Play: Take the South cards now. How will you plan the play when West leads the ♠Q?

You can hope to make tricks with all four of your honor cards. If you can add four trump tricks in dummy, all will end well. You win with the ♠A and ruff a spade in dummy. When you lead a diamond, East plays low and your ◊K wins. After ruffing another spade in dummy, you finesse the ♡Q successfully. You continue with a third spade ruff, East following suit. A heart to the ace is followed by a heart ruff, the fourth trump trick, and you then have eight tricks.

If East had been able to overruff the third round of hearts, there would be some chance that you would score the ♣K subsequently.

PLAY DEAL 17-3

N-S Vul. Dealer West

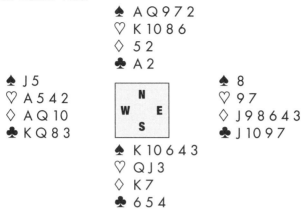

```
                    ♠ A Q 9 7 2
                    ♡ K 10 8 6
                    ◇ 5 2
                    ♣ A 2
 ♠ J 5                              ♠ 8
 ♡ A 5 4 2          N               ♡ 9 7
 ◇ A Q 10       W       E           ◇ J 9 8 6 4 3
 ♣ K Q 8 3          S               ♣ J 10 9 7
                    ♠ K 10 6 4 3
                    ♡ Q J 3
                    ◇ K 7
                    ♣ 6 5 4
```

West	North	East	South
1NT	2♣	pass	3♠
pass	4♠	all pass	

The Bidding: North enters the auction with a Landy 2♣, showing a hand that is at least 5-4 in the majors. With five-card spade support and some useful cards, South invites a game by jumping to 3♠. North is happy to make it 4♠.

The Play: West leads the ♣K against the spade game. What is your plan?

Suppose you win the first trick with the ♣A, draw trumps and play a heart, hoping to set up a discard for one of your diamond losers. Do you see what may go wrong?

East will play the ♣J at Trick 1 to tell his partner that he holds the ♣J10. In other words, he will let West know that he can cross to the East hand with a club. (If East held ♣J954 instead, he would encourage with the ♣9 to show the ♣J as an entry.) When West won with the ♡A, he would be able to cross to partner's hand by leading a low club. East would switch to a diamond through your king and that would be one down.

You can prevent this outcome with a simple move that costs you absolutely nothing. You allow the ♣K to win the first trick! You win the next club, draw trumps and set up the hearts. West cannot cross to his partner's hand, so you will be able to discard a diamond on the fourth round of hearts.

PLAY DEAL 17-4

N-S Vul. Dealer East

```
              ♠ A K 2
              ♡ J 10 4
              ◇ Q J 8 2
              ♣ A 4 3
  ♠ 6                        ♠ Q J 8 4
  ♡ 8 6 3 2        N         ♡ K 7
  ◇ 10 7 6 4 3   W   E       ◇ K 9 5
  ♣ 10 9 5         S         ♣ K Q J 7
              ♠ 10 9 7 5 3
              ♡ A Q 9 5
              ◇ A
              ♣ 8 6 2
```

West	North	East	South
		1NT	2♣
pass	3♣	pass	3♠
pass	4♠	all pass	

The Bidding: When South bids a Landy 2♣, North wants to play at the game-level in partner's five-card suit. He responds 3♣, a special bid to discover which five-card major partner has. When South rebids 3♠, North raises to 4♠.

The Play: West leads the ♣10. How would you play the contract?

You and your partner hold 25 HCP between you, so East must hold all the missing honor cards to make up his 1NT opening bid. The heart finesse will win — you know that — but your two potential club losers may still be accompanied by two trump losers, if the suit breaks 4-1. To guard against this situation, you must aim to dispose of a club loser on dummy's diamond suit.

You win with the ♣A, cross to the ◇A and return to dummy with the ♠K. You then lead the ◇Q for a ruffing finesse. If East follows with a low diamond, you will discard a club loser. When instead he covers with the ◇K, you ruff in your hand. You then return to dummy with the ♠A, West showing out, and discard a club loser on the established ◇J. Next you turn to the heart suit, leading the ♡J for a finesse. You will lose two trumps and one club, making your game.

SOPHISTICATED

3

STUFF

LEBENSOHL 2NT

Suppose partner opens 1NT and the next player overcalls 2♠. There are two possible meanings for your new-suit bid of 3◇. One is 'natural and forcing'. The other is 'I would like to compete in 3◇; please pass.'

The Lebensohl convention gives you the best of both worlds. If you bid a new suit directly (3♣, 3◇ or 3♡) this is game-forcing. If instead you bid 2NT, this is the Lebensohl convention. Partner is required to rebid 3♣ and you can then either pass or make a sign-off bid in one of the red suits.

You	LHO	Partner	RHO	You
♠ 5 4		1NT	2♠	2NT
♡ Q J 8 5 4 2	pass	3♣	pass	3♡
◇ 9 5				
♣ Q 6 3				

An immediate 3♡ would have been forcing. Since you bid a Lebensohl 2NT first, your 3♡ merely contests the partscore. It is weak, and partner should pass.

Sometimes there is space for three options. After 1NT and a 2♡ overcall, you can sign off in 2♠, jump to 3♠ on a game-forcing hand and bid 3♠ via a Lebensohl 2NT to invite a game.

There are also four strong sequences when your hand is fairly balanced. After 1NT and a 2♠ overcall, you can choose between:

2NT and then 3♣	Stayman for hearts, including a spade stopper
2NT and then 3NT	To play in 3NT, including a spade stopper
3♠	Stayman for hearts but no spade stopper
3NT	To play in 3NT but no spade stopper

You	LHO	Partner	RHO	You
♠ K 4 2		1NT	2♠	2NT
♡ A J 7 6	pass	3♣	pass	3♠
◇ 8 2				
♣ Q 10 8 2				

Your 2NT followed by 3♠ shows four hearts and a spade stopper.

PLAY DEAL 18-1

E-W Vul. Dealer North

```
                    ♠ K Q 10
                    ♡ Q 9 5
                    ◇ K J 4
                    ♣ A 9 8 2
   ♠ A 9 6 5 2          N           ♠ 8 7 3
   ♡ 10 2                            ♡ A K J 7 6 4
   ◇ Q 7 3          W     E          ◇ 8
   ♣ Q 7 5             S             ♣ K J 3
                    ♠ J 4
                    ♡ 8 3
                    ◇ A 10 9 6 5 2
                    ♣ 10 6 4
```

West	North	East	South
	1NT	2♡	2NT
pass	3♣	pass	3◇
all pass			

The Bidding: With a six-card suit and the knowledge that his side holds at least half the points in the pack, South decides to contest the auction. He bids a Lebensohl 2NT, asking partner to rebid 3♣. With the same values and long clubs, South would have passed 3♣. As it is, he corrects to 3◇, which partner will nearly always pass. (If he held three aces and ◇Kxxx, he might take a punt at 3NT, but this would be an exception to the general rule.)

The Play: West leads the ♡10, East overtaking with the ♡J in case the lead is a singleton. East continues with the ♡A and the ♡K. How will you play the contract?

The ♡9 is in dummy, so you can be sure that West started with only two hearts. You need to guess which defender holds the ◇Q. Since West has several hearts fewer than East, he is a strong favorite to hold more diamonds and therefore the ◇Q. You should therefore ruff the third round of hearts with the ◇A. You then lead the ◇10, running the card (playing low from dummy). After drawing trumps, you establish the spade suit and can then discard a club loser from your hand on the third round of spades. You lose one spade, two hearts and a club, making the contract.

A club switch from East at Trick 3 would have defeated the contract.

PLAY DEAL 18-2

E-W Vul. Dealer South

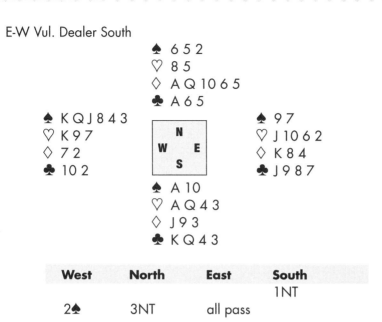

♠ 6 5 2
♡ 8 5
♢ A Q 10 6 5
♣ A 6 5

♠ K Q J 8 4 3
♡ K 9 7
♢ 7 2
♣ 10 2

♠ 9 7
♡ J 10 6 2
♢ K 8 4
♣ J 9 8 7

♠ A 10
♡ A Q 4 3
♢ J 9 3
♣ K Q 4 3

West	North	East	South
			1NT
2♠	3NT	all pass	

The Bidding: When West overcalls 2♠, North bids 3NT directly. What does this mean? When you are playing Lebensohl you have two ways of bidding 3NT — directly or via a Lebensohl 2NT. You also have two ways of bidding a Stayman 3♣ (directly or via Lebensohl). In both cases you start with 2NT when you hold a stopper in the opponent's suit. Here North bid 3NT directly, denying a spade stopper. South passes 3NT because he holds a spade stopper himself. Without one, he would have to bid his lowest suit at the four-level and the partnership would look for some alternative contract.

The Play: How will you play 3NT when West leads the ♠K?

You have six tricks on top and will have to develop the diamonds to give you the contract. All will be easy if West holds the ♢K. If East holds that card, you will have to hope that he has no more spades left when he takes his diamond trick. With this aim in mind, you should hold up the ♠A at Trick 1. You win the spade continuation and, because spades break 6-2, East has no spades left. You run the ♢J into what you hope is now a safe hand. If East ducks, you run the ♢9 next.

When East takes his ♢K, he will switch to a heart. To finesse the ♡Q would be a needless risk and would allow West to win and cash several spade tricks. So, you rise with the ♡A and claim the contract with four diamonds, three clubs and the major-suit aces.

PLAY DEAL 18-3

E-W Vul. Dealer West

```
                    ♠ J 7
                    ♡ A Q 6 4
                    ♢ 9 7 4 2
                    ♣ K 4 3
   ♠ A K Q 8 6 4          ┌─────────┐          ♠ 9 2
   ♡ 9 7                  │    N    │          ♡ J 8 5
   ♢ J 6                  │ W     E │          ♢ Q 10 8 5
   ♣ 9 8 5                │    S    │          ♣ J 10 7 2
                          └─────────┘
                    ♠ 10 5 3
                    ♡ K 10 3 2
                    ♢ A K 3
                    ♣ A Q 6
```

West	North	East	South
			1NT
2♠	3♠	pass	4♡
all pass			

The Bidding: North has 10 HCPs, enough for game opposite your 15-17 point 1NT. He wants to play either in 3NT, if you have a spade stopper, or in 4♡ if you have a four-card heart fit for him. He bids 3♠ directly, to deny a spade stopper and ask whether you hold four hearts. If instead he had bid a 'Slow Shows' 2NT and then bid 3♠, he would still have asked for a four-card heart fit but he would have told you that he did have a spade stopper. South shows his heart fit by bidding 4♡.

The Play: West leads the ♠A and ♠K, East playing the ♠9 and then the ♠2 to show his doubleton. How will you play the heart game when West continues with the ♠Q?

If you ruff with a low trump in dummy, it is clear that East will overruff and an eventual diamond loser will put you one down. Instead you must ruff with the ♡Q (or ♡A). Now that your trump holding has been weakened, you must pick up the ♡J. It is a better chance to finesse East for ♡Jxx than to hope to drop the ♡J in two rounds with five cards missing. That is particularly the case here because West has many more spades than East and is therefore likely to be shorter than him in hearts. You play the ♡A, finesse the ♡10 successfully and draw the last trump with your ♡K. The contract is then yours.

PLAY DEAL 18-4

Both Vul. Dealer North

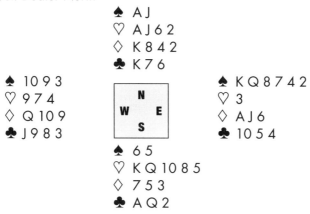

```
              ♠ A J
              ♡ A J 6 2
              ◊ K 8 4 2
              ♣ K 7 6
♠ 10 9 3                        ♠ K Q 8 7 4 2
♡ 9 7 4          N             ♡ 3
◊ Q 10 9     W       E         ◊ A J 6
♣ J 9 8 3        S             ♣ 10 5 4
              ♠ 6 5
              ♡ K Q 10 8 5
              ◊ 7 5 3
              ♣ A Q 2
```

West	North	East	South
	1NT	2♠	3♡
pass	4♡	all pass	

The Bidding: South is strong enough for game and chooses a forcing 3♡ as his response. (On a weaker hand with five or six hearts, he might choose to bid a Lebensohl 2NT, intending to bid 3♡ over partner's expected 3♣.) North is very happy to raise the hearts and there is no further bidding.

The Play: How would you play this contract when West leads the ♠10? It may seem that you will need West to hold the ◊A but there is a clever way to ensure the contract even when East holds that card. You win the spade lead and draw trumps in three rounds. You continue with three rounds of clubs and then play the ♠J. It is no surprise (after the bidding and West's opening lead of the ♠10) when East has to win this trick.

Poor East will now have to assist you. If he plays a diamond, you will score an extra trick with dummy's ◊K. If instead East plays a third round of spades, this will give you a ruff-and-sluff. You will be able to ruff with dummy's last trump and discard a diamond loser from your hand. Either way the contract is yours.

You may have noticed that an inspired (and very unlikely) diamond lead would give the defenders a chance to beat the contract. Taking three diamond tricks would set up dummy's ◊K for a spade discard. The defenders would have to take just two diamond tricks and then switch to spades, setting up their fourth trick in time.

REVERSE DRURY

When partner opens 1♡ or 1♠ in third or fourth seat, you may get too high if you make an invitational bid (traditionally by raising to the three-level). Particularly in third seat, partner may have opened a hand that is short of the normal values. Playing the Reverse Drury convention, you can respond with an artificial 2♣ to ask partner how strong his hand is:

LHO	Partner	RHO	You
			pass
pass	1♡ or 1♠	pass	2♣

Your 2♣ here is Reverse Drury. It says nothing about clubs but guarantees at least three cards in partner's major and a maximum pass (10+ HCP).

Partner	You		
pass	1♠	♠	K Q J 9 8
2♣	2♠	♡	10 3
		◇	9 7
		♣	K 10 5 4

You open with 9 HCP in third seat, hoping at least to get a spade lead if they outbid you. Imagine how you would hate it if partner responded 3♠ now! Instead he responds with a Reverse Drury 2♣. With a sound opening bid, you would rebid with an artificial 2◇ and the bidding would proceed naturally. As you are very weak, you rebid 2♠. Warned not to go too high, partner passes and you stop at the two-level.

Partner	You		
pass	1♡	♠	3
2♣	4♡	♡	A K J 5 4
		◇	K Q 9 5
		♣	K 10 4

Sometimes opener can place the final contract immediately. Here you happily bid 4♡ when you hear of heart support and 10+ points opposite.

What if you, as responder, hold 10 points and five or six clubs? Well, you have given up the natural 2♣ response and must find another bid, perhaps 1NT or a natural 3♣. Both these responses would deny three-card support for partner's suit.

PLAY DEAL 19-1

E-W Vul. Dealer North.

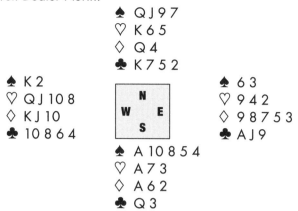

```
                        ♠ Q J 9 7
                        ♡ K 6 5
                        ◇ Q 4
                        ♣ K 7 5 2
    ♠ K 2                                  ♠ 6 3
    ♡ Q J 10 8            N                ♡ 9 4 2
    ◇ K J 10         W         E           ◇ 9 8 7 5 3
    ♣ 10 8 6 4           S                 ♣ A J 9
                        ♠ A 10 8 5 4
                        ♡ A 7 3
                        ◇ A 6 2
                        ♣ Q 3
```

West	North	East	South
	pass	pass	1♠
pass	2♣	pass	2◇
pass	3♠	pass	4♠
all pass			

The Bidding: South opens 1♠ in the third seat. North has no wish to leap immediately to 3♠ in case his partner has made a light opening. He bids 2♣, Reverse Drury. South has a sound opening bid and indicates this by rebidding 2◇. North is too good to bid just 2♠ at his second turn. With four-card support and 11 HCP facing a sound opening bid, he is worth 3♠. South is then happy to advance to game.

The Play: West leads the ♡Q. How would you play the contract?

Suppose you win with dummy's ♡K and run the ♠Q. You will make the contract when the finesse wins. If it loses, West will clear the heart suit. You will then lose a further trick in each side suit and go down.

A better idea is to combine two chances. You win the first trick with the ♡A and lead a low diamond towards the queen. West rises with the ◇K and persists with another heart to dummy's king. You play the ◇Q and return to your hand with the ♠A. (To take a trump finesse would cost the contract.) You can then discard dummy's last heart on the ◇A and play a second round of trumps. By avoiding a heart loser, you make the contract.

Suppose the ◇Q had lost to the ◇K with East. You would then have had to rely on the trump finesse for the contract.

PLAY DEAL 19-2

E-W Vul. Dealer North.

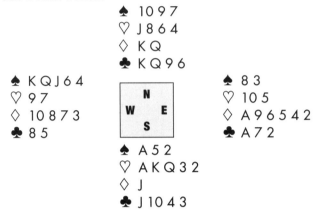

```
                    ♠ 10 9 7
                    ♡ J 8 6 4
                    ◇ K Q
                    ♣ K Q 9 6
♠ K Q J 6 4                          ♠ 8 3
♡ 9 7              N                 ♡ 10 5
◇ 10 8 7 3      W     E              ◇ A 9 6 5 4 2
♣ 8 5              S                 ♣ A 7 2
                    ♠ A 5 2
                    ♡ A K Q 3 2
                    ◇ J
                    ♣ J 10 4 3
```

West	North	East	South
	pass	pass	1♡
pass	2♣	pass	4♡
all pass			

The Bidding: South opens 1♡ in the third seat. West would like to show his spades but he is nervous of overcalling 1♠ when vulnerable and holding such a weak hand. North announces a good heart raise with his Drury 2♣. South likes his hand and goes directly to 4♡.

The Play: How will you play 4♡ when West leads the ♠K? You hold a combined total of 26 HCP but prospects are poor. It seems that you are almost certain to lose two spades and the minor-suit aces. Can you see any chance of making ten tricks?

You must hope that West is leading from a five-card spade suit and that East holds both the missing aces. Not much of a chance but better than none! You hold up your ♠A on the first round. You win the second round of spades, hoping that East now has no spades left, and draw trumps in two rounds. Then you lead the ◇J to set up a diamond winner for a discard. East wins with the ◇A and has no spade to play, thanks to your hold-up in the suit. What's more, he also holds the ♣A and cannot therefore cross to his partner's hand in the suit. Magic! Nothing can prevent you from crossing to dummy subsequently and discarding your last spade on the ◇K.

PLAY DEAL 19-3

E-W Vul. Dealer North.

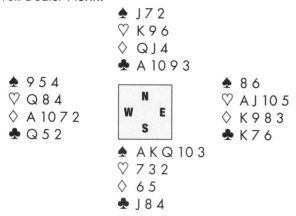

```
                    ♠ J 7 2
                    ♥ K 9 6
                    ◇ Q J 4
                    ♣ A 10 9 3
    ♠ 9 5 4                        ♠ 8 6
    ♥ Q 8 4         N              ♥ A J 10 5
    ◇ A 10 7 2    W   E            ◇ K 9 8 3
    ♣ Q 5 2         S              ♣ K 7 6
                    ♠ A K Q 10 3
                    ♥ 7 3 2
                    ◇ 6 5
                    ♣ J 8 4
```

West	North	East	South
	pass	pass	1♠
pass	2♣	pass	2♠
all pass			

The Bidding: South opens his moderate hand in the third seat, bidding 1♠. North has 11 HCP and three-card spade support, but is wary of reaching the three-level in case his partner has opened light. He shows his values with a Drury 2♣. South's 2♠ announces that he has a minimum, or sub-minimum, opening and the bidding stops there.

The Play: Even 2♠ is at risk if the defenders are on their toes. Declarer wins the trump lead and draws trumps in two further rounds. He then leads a club to the ten, hoping to develop that suit. East wins with the ♣K and sees that five tricks will be needed in the red suits to beat the contract. He switches to a low diamond, which West wins with the ace. What should West do now?

Returning a diamond would be a poor idea, since East would not be able to play hearts effectively after winning with the ◇K. Instead, West should switch to the ♥Q. After this sparkling defense the defenders would score three hearts, two diamonds and a club, putting 2♠ one down.

Losing 50 on the North-South cards is not such a bad result, since East-West could have made nine tricks in diamonds (discarding a club loser on the fourth round of hearts).

PLAY DEAL 19-4

Neither Vul. Dealer North.

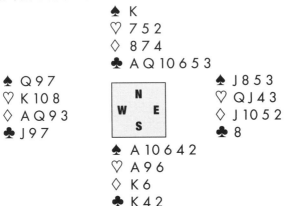

```
                    ♠ K
                    ♡ 7 5 2
                    ◇ 8 7 4
                    ♣ A Q 10 6 5 3
    ♠ Q 9 7                           ♠ J 8 5 3
    ♡ K 10 8          N              ♡ Q J 4 3
    ◇ A Q 9 3      W     E           ◇ J 10 5 2
    ♣ J 9 7           S              ♣ 8
                    ♠ A 10 6 4 2
                    ♡ A 9 6
                    ◇ K 6
                    ♣ K 4 2
```

West	North	East	South
	pass	pass	1♠
pass	3♣	pass	3NT
all pass			

The Bidding: South opens 1♠ in the third seat. What should North respond? He cannot bid 2♣ because this would be Drury. He has to choose between 1NT and 3♣. With six pretty good clubs, he prefers the bid in this suit. Although there is no certainty about it, South sees a fair chance of making 3NT. This is the bid he chooses and that closes the auction.

The Play: Once you have managed to bid 3NT, there will be no problems in the play. West has an unattractive lead to make. When he eventually makes up his mind, you will be able to claim at least six clubs, two spades and one heart.

ROMAN KEYCARD BLACKWOOD

For many decades most players used regular Blackwood, asking how many of the four aces partner held. Then a new version of Blackwood became popular, one that allows you to discover whether partner holds the king of trumps and even the queen of trumps. The new responses to a 4NT enquiry refer to five 'keycards'. These are the four aces and, just as important, the king of trumps. Suppose the bidding starts:

Partner	You
1♡	3♡
4NT	?

Your heart raise sets that suit as trumps and partner's Roman Keycard Blackwood asks you how many of the five keycards you hold. You will respond on these lines:

5♣	1 or 4 keycards[1]
5♢	0 or 3 keycards
5♡	2 keycards, *without* the queen of trumps
5♠	2 keycards, *with* the queen of trumps.

When partner has responded 5♣ or 5♢, you may bid the cheapest non-trump suit to ask if he holds the queen of trumps.

Partner	You
1♡	3♡
4NT	5♣
5♢	?

Partner is asking about the ♡Q. You sign off in 5♡ without it and show your lowest side-suit king (for example 5♠ to show the ♠K) when you do hold the ♡Q. With the ♡Q and no side-suit king, you bid 5NT.

If instead partner follows his 4NT with 5NT, this asks how many side-suit kings you hold (6♣=0, 6♢=1, 6♡=2, 6♠=3). Do not include the trump king because your previous response already dealt with that card.

---

1. This method (1430) is the most popular. However, some use 3014, reversing the meanings of the 5♣ and 5♢ responses. Discuss this with your partner.

PLAY DEAL 20-1

N-S Vul. Dealer South.

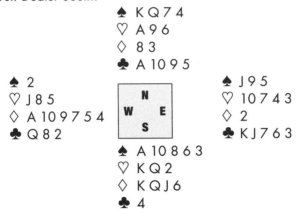

```
                    ♠ K Q 7 4
                    ♡ A 9 6
                    ◇ 8 3
                    ♣ A 10 9 5
   ♠ 2                              ♠ J 9 5
   ♡ J 8 5            N             ♡ 10 7 4 3
   ◇ A 10 9 7 5 4   W   E           ◇ 2
   ♣ Q 8 2            S             ♣ K J 7 6 3
                    ♠ A 10 8 6 3
                    ♡ K Q 2
                    ◇ K Q J 6
                    ♣ 4
```

West	North	East	South
			1♠
pass	2NT	pass	4NT
pass	5◇	pass	6♠
pass	all pass		

The Bidding: North bids Jacoby 2NT (see Chapter 9) to show a sound raise to at least 4♠. South then decides that he is willing to play in a slam if North holds sufficient keycards. The 5◇ response shows three keycards and South decides to bid a small slam. If North holds the three side-suit aces, there will be an excellent chance of losing at most one trump trick. If instead North holds two aces and the ♠K, the slam will depend on a 2-2 trump break at worst.

The Play: In the face of such confident bidding, West decides that the best chance of beating the contract is to give his partner a ruff. He leads the ◇A and East follows with the ◇2. (Declarer may follow with the ◇K or ◇Q in an attempt to convince West that he is short in diamonds.) West should continue with a second round of the suit, since no other defense offers a practical chance of beating the slam. East duly ruffs the second round of diamonds and the slam goes one down.

PLAY DEAL 20-2

E-W Vul. Dealer South.

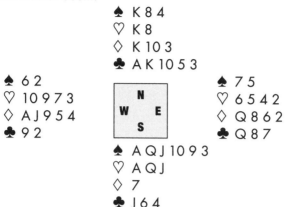

♠ K 8 4
♡ K 8
◇ K 10 3
♣ A K 10 5 3

♠ 6 2
♡ 10 9 7 3
◇ A J 9 5 4
♣ 9 2

♠ 7 5
♡ 6 5 4 2
◇ Q 8 6 2
♣ Q 8 7

♠ A Q J 10 9 3
♡ A Q J
◇ 7
♣ J 6 4

West	North	East	South
			1♠
pass	2♣	pass	3♠
pass	4NT	pass	5♠
pass	6♠	all pass	

The Bidding: North's RKCB 4NT agrees spades as trumps and asks for key-cards. When South shows two keycards and the ♠Q, North bids 6♠.

The Play: How will you play 6♠ when West leads the ♡10?

You start with one potential loser in each minor suit. What chances do you have of avoiding one of them? If West holds the ♣Q, a finesse in that suit will give you the slam. There's no need to rely solely on that because you can lead towards dummy's ◇K first. When West holds the ◇A, he must concede the contract. If he rises with the ace, you will have a discard for your club loser on dummy's ◇K. If instead West plays low, you will not lose a diamond trick and can afford to lose a club trick.

If the ◇K loses to the ◇A with East, then your best chance in clubs is to finesse West for the queen. You should play the ♣A on the first round, just in case East has a singleton ♣Q.

Both Vul. Dealer South.

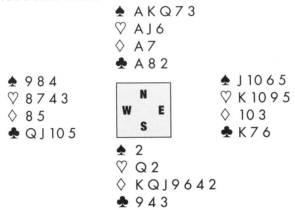

```
                    ♠ A K Q 7 3
                    ♡ A J 6
                    ◇ A 7
                    ♣ A 8 2
  ♠ 9 8 4                              ♠ J 10 6 5
  ♡ 8 7 4 3          N                 ♡ K 10 9 5
  ◇ 8 5           W     E              ◇ 10 3
  ♣ Q J 10 5         S                 ♣ K 7 6
                    ♠ 2
                    ♡ Q 2
                    ◇ K Q J 9 6 4 2
                    ♣ 9 4 3
```

West	North	East	South
			3◇
pass	4NT	pass	5♣
pass	5♡	pass	5NT
pass	7◇	all pass	

The Bidding: When North hears a 3◇ opening from partner, he is happy to make diamonds trumps. Since he intends to ask whether partner holds the ◇K and ◇Q, he bids a RKCB 4NT immediately, rather than confuse the auction by bidding his spades. 5♣ shows one keycard (the ◇K) and 5♡, the cheapest non-trump bid, then asks for the ◇Q. To deny this card, South would sign off in 6◇. 5NT means: 'Yes, I have the ◇Q but no side-suit king.' North then bids 7◇.

The Play: You win West's ♣Q lead in the dummy. What is your plan for thirteen tricks?

You have twelve top tricks. There are two chances for a thirteenth trick. If spades break 4-3, one spade ruff will establish the suit. If spades break unkindly, you can fall back on the heart finesse. You draw trumps and play dummy's three top spades, throwing your two club losers. When both defenders follow all the way, you know that the spade suit will yield the extra trick that you need. You ruff a spade in your hand, bringing down East's ♠J, and return to dummy with the ♡A. You can then discard the ♡Q on the established long card in spades.

If spades had broken 5-2 or worse, you would have had to take a successful finesse in hearts to make the grand slam.

PLAY DEAL 20-4

E-W Vul. Dealer North.

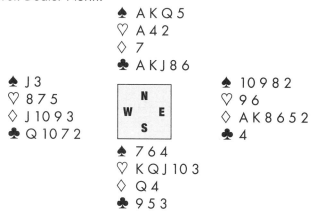

                 ♠ A K Q 5
                 ♡ A 4 2
                 ◇ 7
                 ♣ A K J 8 6

♠ J 3   ♠ 10 9 8 2
♡ 8 7 5   N   ♡ 9 6
◇ J 10 9 3   W   E   ◇ A K 8 6 5 2
♣ Q 10 7 2   S   ♣ 4

                 ♠ 7 6 4
                 ♡ K Q J 10 3
                 ◇ Q 4
                 ♣ 9 5 3

West	North	East	South
	2♣	pass	2♡
pass	4NT	pass	5♣
pass	5◇	pass	5NT
pass	6♡	all pass	

The Bidding: South makes a positive response in hearts, showing a good suit and 8+ HCP. North then sees no purpose in bidding his own suits; he has already found a great trump fit in hearts. RKCB places South with one keycard (the ♡K) and North then asks for the ♡Q by making the cheapest non-trump bid of 5◇. South's 5NT shows the trump queen but no side-suit king.

The Play: How would you play 6♡ when West leads the ◇J to the ◇K, East switching to the ♠10?

You win in the dummy and lead a low trump to the king. You then ruff the ◇Q with the ♡A. This allows you to return to your hand with the ♡4 to the ♡Q. After drawing the last trump, you must give yourself the best chance of avoiding a club loser. How would you continue?

You should play dummy's three top spades to see if the suit breaks 3-3. If it does, you will be able to discard a club on the fourth round of spades. As the cards lie, East will show up with a spade stopper. You cash the ♣A, just in case East holds a singleton ♣Q, and then return to your hand by ruffing the fourth round of spades. Your final chance, a finesse of the ♣J, proves successful and the slam is yours.

FOURTH SUIT FORCING

One of the most valuable conventions in constructive bidding is 'fourth suit forcing'. When the bidding starts with bids in three suits (for example, 1◇ – 1♠ – 2♣), the responder can make an artificial bid in the fourth suit (2♡ on the sequence mentioned). What does such a bid mean?
- I am strong enough for a game contract (at least)
- Please continue to describe your hand

You	You	Partner
♠ A 8 7		1◇
♡ K Q 10 7 4	1♡	1♠
◇ A 9	2♣*	
♣ 10 5 3		

You are strong enough for a game contract but have no idea so far what game will be best. It might be 3NT, 4♡, 4♠ or conceivably 5◇! Your fourth-suit forcing bid of 2♣ asks for further information. It says nothing about your clubs. Usually you will not have a good holding in that suit or you would have been able to head for 3NT.

If partner bids 2NT next, showing a club stopper, you will raise to 3NT. If he bids 2♡ or 3♡, you will bid 4♡. If he rebids his spades, you will raise to 4♠. If he can only say 2◇, you will continue with 2♡ (still game-forcing, of course) and you can investigate where to play at your leisure.

You should check with your partner but many players like to make one exception to the idea that a bid in the fourth suit is artificial:

Partner	You
1♣	1◇
1♡	1♠

If you decide that 1♠ should be natural (an exception to the rule), then you will have to use a bid of 2♠ as fourth suit forcing.

When you hold a two-suiter in your first-bid suit and the unbid suit, you can jump in the second suit. 1◇ – 1♠ – 2♣ – 3♡ would show at least 5-5 in the major suits (game forcing).

PLAY DEAL 21-1

Neither Vul. Dealer South.

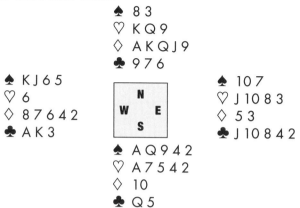

```
                    ♠ 8 3
                    ♡ K Q 9
                    ◇ A K Q J 9
                    ♣ 9 7 6
   ♠ K J 6 5                        ♠ 10 7
   ♡ 6              N               ♡ J 10 8 3
   ◇ 8 7 6 4 2    W   E             ◇ 5 3
   ♣ A K 3          S               ♣ J 10 8 4 2
                    ♠ A Q 9 4 2
                    ♡ A 7 5 4 2
                    ◇ 10
                    ♣ Q 5
```

West	North	East	South
			1♠
pass	2◇	pass	2♡
pass	3♣	pass	3♡
pass	4♡	all pass	

The Bidding: North is strong enough for a game contract but he has no idea which game contract it should be. He bids a fourth-suit-forcing 3♣. When South rebids his hearts, an eight-card fit has been found. North raises to game.

The Play: West leads the ♣A and ♣K, dropping declarer's queen on the second round. He continues with the ♣3, East playing the ♣10. How will you play the contract after this start?

You ruff the third club. If hearts break 3-2, you will be able to draw trumps and score five diamond tricks for an overtrick. What will happen if a defender holds four trumps? You cannot simply draw three rounds and then start on the diamonds; the defender would ruff at some stage and there would be no way back to dummy. Nor could you concede a fourth round of trumps before playing on diamonds. You would then have no trumps left and the defenders might score a club trick or two.

You should test the trumps by playing the king and ace. If everyone follows, you will draw the last trump and claim an overtrick. When West shows out on the second trump, you abandon trumps and run the diamonds. When East ruffs, you will win his return and cross to dummy with the ♡Q, drawing East's last trump. You can then score the remaining diamonds.

PLAY DEAL 21-2

Both Vul. Dealer North.

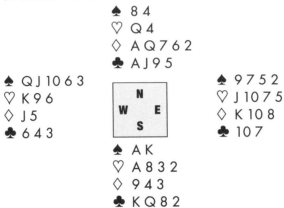

```
                    ♠ 8 4
                    ♡ Q 4
                    ◇ A Q 7 6 2
                    ♣ A J 9 5
   ♠ Q J 10 6 3                          ♠ 9 7 5 2
   ♡ K 9 6            N                   ♡ J 10 7 5
   ◇ J 5          W       E               ◇ K 10 8
   ♣ 6 4 3            S                   ♣ 10 7
                    ♠ A K
                    ♡ A 8 3 2
                    ◇ 9 4 3
                    ♣ K Q 8 2
```

West	North	East	South
	1◇	pass	1♡
pass	2♣	pass	2♠
pass	3◇	pass	3NT
all pass			

The Bidding: North's 2♣ covers a wide range of points (around 12-18) because a jump to 3♣ would be game-forcing. South has 16 points and a club fit, so it would be pessimistic to bid only 3NT at his second turn. He asks for further information with his fourth-suit 2♠. North has no support for hearts, nor a stopper in the fourth suit (spades). Although he has suggested five diamonds with his bidding so far, he has little alternative but to bid 3◇. South then bids 3NT, leaving any move towards a slam to his partner.

The Play: The ♠Q is led and you count eight top tricks. Suppose your next move is to finesse the ◇Q. You will go down! East will clear the spades and it will be too late for you to lead towards the ♡Q, seeking your ninth trick there; the defenders would claim three spades, one heart and one diamond.

Since playing on hearts will result in losing the lead even if West holds the ♡K, you should go for this chance first. Let's say that West rises with the ♡K and clears the spade suit. Nine tricks are yours. If East had held the ♡K, proceeding to clear the spades, you would still have been able to take the diamond finesse. By playing hearts first, you give yourself two chances to make the contract instead of one!

PLAY DEAL 21-3

N-S Vul. Dealer South.

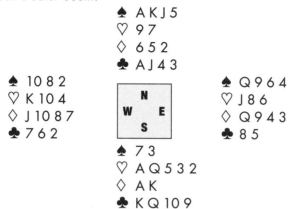

```
              ♠ A K J 5
              ♡ 9 7
              ◇ 6 5 2
              ♣ A J 4 3
♠ 10 8 2                      ♠ Q 9 6 4
♡ K 10 4         N           ♡ J 8 6
◇ J 10 8 7    W     E        ◇ Q 9 4 3
♣ 7 6 2          S           ♣ 8 5
              ♠ 7 3
              ♡ A Q 5 3 2
              ◇ A K
              ♣ K Q 10 9
```

West	North	East	South
			1♡
pass	1♠	pass	2♣
pass	2◇	pass	2NT
pass	3♣	pass	4NT
pass	5♡	pass	6♣
all pass			

The Bidding: North is too strong for a non-forcing raise of 2♣ to 3♣. He bids a fourth-suit 2◇, intending to bid 3♣ on the next round if possible. Since 2◇ is game-forcing, South can bid just 2NT on his hand and wait to see what partner has in mind. This allows North to show his game-forcing raise in clubs. If South had a minimum opening, he could offer 3NT now. With his splendid four-loser 18-count, he decides to head for a slam.

The Play: How will you play 6♣ when West leads the ◇J?

You win with the ◇A, cross to the ♠A and finesse the ♡Q, tackling your main side suit immediately. The finesse loses and you win West's diamond continuation. All follow to the ♡A and you ruff a third round of hearts with dummy's ♣J. When the heart suit breaks 3-3, there will be no need for a further heart ruff. You draw trumps and claim the contract.

PLAY DEAL 21-4

E-W Vul. Dealer South.

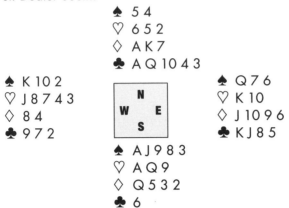

```
                    ♠ 5 4
                    ♡ 6 5 2
                    ◇ A K 7
                    ♣ A Q 10 4 3
    ♠ K 10 2                        ♠ Q 7 6
    ♡ J 8 7 4 3        N           ♡ K 10
    ◇ 8 4         W         E      ◇ J 10 9 6
    ♣ 9 7 2           S            ♣ K J 8 5
                    ♠ A J 9 8 3
                    ♡ A Q 9
                    ◇ Q 5 3 2
                    ♣ 6
```

West	North	East	South
			1♠
pass	2♣	pass	2◇
pass	2♡	pass	3NT
all pass			

The Bidding: North has no good natural bid to make over 2◇. He cannot bid 3NT with only three spot cards in hearts. Thank goodness for fourth suit forcing! He bids 2♡ and South jumps to 3NT. This does not show any extra values because 2NT would have been forcing. What it does show is a double stopper in the fourth suit. In other words it tells partner that 3NT is very likely to be the best contract from what South can see.

The Play: How will you play 3NT when West leads the ♡4 and East plays the ♡K? You have seven top tricks after the heart lead and the spade suit offers the best prospects of two more. You cross to the ◇A and lead a spade to the nine. West wins with the ♠10, you are disappointed to see, and continues with the ♡3 to East's ♡10. What now?

West led the ♡4 and then played the ♡3, so he began with a five-card suit. The ♡10 is East's last heart! You must allow this card to win. Poor East cannot continue hearts and you still have a stopper in the suit. Let's say that East switches to the ◇J. You win with dummy's ◇K and play a spade to the ace. (This will give you the contract when spades are 3-3 or West began with ♠K10 or ♠Q10.) You then play a third round of spades, setting up two extra winners in the suit. The game is yours.

NEW MINOR FORCING

We have already seen that there are plenty of sequences available to find the best contract after partner has opened 1NT. 'New minor forcing' is a convention that allows you similar flexibility when partner has rebid 1NT.

(1)	**Partner**	**You**		**(2)**	**Partner**	**You**
	1♣	1♡			1♢	1♠
	1NT (12-14)	2♢*			1NT (12-14)	2♣ *

In both sequences the starred bid asks for further information. The bid is not game-forcing but it is always at least invitational (11+ HCP).

The opener's continuations *in order of priority* are:

1. Show an unbid four-card major.
2. Support partner's major with three trumps.
3. With a minimum and no support for partner's major, bid 2NT. If partner has only invitational values, he will pass.
4. With a maximum and no support for partner's major, bid 3NT.

Partner		**Partner**	**You**
♠ A J 2		1♣	1♡
♡ K 9 4		1NT	2♢
♢ 8 5 3		2♡	
♣ A 10 8 4			

Your partner rebids 2♡, showing three-card heart support and a minimum hand. Add the ♣Q to the hand and he would bid 3♡ instead.

Partner		**Partner**	**You**
♠ Q 8 4		1♢	1♠
♡ A Q 6 2		1NT	2♣
♢ Q J 9 3		3♡	3NT
♣ K 5		4♠	

Since you did not hold four hearts, partner knows you must have five spades.

N-S Vul. Dealer South.

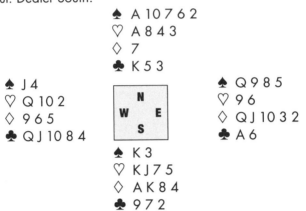

♠ A 10 7 6 2
♡ A 8 4 3
◇ 7
♣ K 5 3

♠ J 4
♡ Q 10 2
◇ 9 6 5
♣ Q J 10 8 4

♠ Q 9 8 5
♡ 9 6
◇ Q J 10 3 2
♣ A 6

♠ K 3
♡ K J 7 5
◇ A K 8 4
♣ 9 7 2

West	North	East	South
			1◇
pass	1♠	pass	1NT
pass	2♣	pass	3♡
pass	4♡	all pass	

The Bidding: When North hears a 1NT rebid he needs to discover whether the partnership has an eight-card fit in one of the major suits. Bidding 2♡ is non-forcing opposite a 1NT response (even though it is a bid in a new suit) and North is worth at least a game try. He therefore uses the 'new minor forcing' convention, bidding 2♣. South must now show his four-card heart suit. Since he has a maximum hand within the 12-14 point range and partner has shown at least invitational strength, South responds 3♡ instead of 2♡. North is then happy to raise to game.

The Play: West leads the ♣Q. Such a lead would be unthinkable if West held the ♣A, so this card can be placed with East. Declarer ducks the first two rounds of clubs in the dummy, just in case East began with a doubleton ♣A. Lo and behold, this comes to pass! East wins the second round of clubs with the ace and switches to the ◇Q. Declarer wins with the ◇A and must now draw trumps. Suppose he crosses to the ♡A and finesses the ♡J (making the best play for no trump losers). This would be a mistake. West might win with an originally doubleton ♡Q and give East a club ruff. West might also win with the ♡Q and return a trump, leaving you with a diamond loser. It is better to play the king and ace of trumps. You ruff your two diamond losers in dummy, losing just two clubs and one trump to make the contract.

PLAY DEAL 22-2

Both Vul. Dealer South.

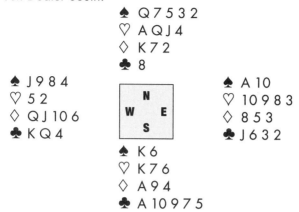

```
                    ♠ Q 7 5 3 2
                    ♡ A Q J 4
                    ◇ K 7 2
                    ♣ 8
  ♠ J 9 8 4                          ♠ A 10
  ♡ 5 2          ┌──────────┐       ♡ 10 9 8 3
  ◇ Q J 10 6     │    N     │       ◇ 8 5 3
  ♣ K Q 4        │ W      E │       ♣ J 6 3 2
                 │    S     │
                 └──────────┘
                    ♠ K 6
                    ♡ K 7 6
                    ◇ A 9 4
                    ♣ A 10 9 7 5
```

West	North	East	South
			1♣
pass	1♠	pass	1NT
pass	2◇	pass	3NT
all pass			

The Bidding: South rebids 1NT to show 12-14 points. North cannot rebid 2♡ because this would be non-forcing opposite a 1NT rebid. He uses a 'new minor forcing' 2◇ to look for an eight-card fit in one of the majors. South has neither three spades nor four hearts. What should he rebid? Since he has a stopper in both red suits, he is happy to bid notrump. Remembering that his partner will have at least game-try values for his 2◇ enquiry, South rebids 3NT instead of 2NT. His hand is a maximum within the range of 12-14.

The Play: How would you play 3NT when West leads the ◇Q? You have seven top tricks, with an easy eighth trick coming in spades. You should aim to score one further trick from the spade suit. You win with dummy's ◇K and lead a low spade to the king. When this wins, you expect East to hold the ♠A. You continue with the ♠6 and play low in the dummy. (There is no point in playing the ♠Q, since East would then win with the ♠A.)

As it happens, East began with only two spades and has to win with the ♠A over dummy's low card. The ♠Q is then good for your ninth trick. If the ♠A did not appear on the second round and the defenders played another diamond, you would have to hope that spades were 3-3 and you could score a second spade trick before the defenders made five tricks their way.

PLAY DEAL 22-3

E-W Vul. Dealer North.

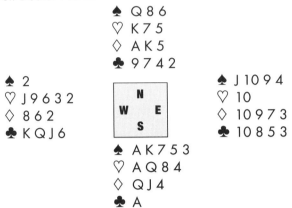

```
                    ♠ Q 8 6
                    ♡ K 7 5
                    ◇ A K 5
                    ♣ 9 7 4 2
♠ 2                                    ♠ J 10 9 4
♡ J 9 6 3 2          N                 ♡ 10
◇ 8 6 2          W       E             ◇ 10 9 7 3
♣ K Q J 6            S                 ♣ 10 8 5 3
                    ♠ A K 7 5 3
                    ♡ A Q 8 4
                    ◇ Q J 4
                    ♣ A
```

West	North	East	South
	1♣	pass	1♠
pass	1NT	pass	2◇
pass	2♠	pass	6♠
all pass			

The Bidding: When South hears a 1NT rebid he needs to discover whether the partnership has an eight-card fit in one of the major suits. How can he do this? Right, he can use the 'new minor forcing' convention, bidding 2◇. North duly shows his three-card spade support. South should probably go through the motions with Roman Keycard Blackwood now (see Chapter 20), but he is a macho six-footer and leaps straight to 6♠. How impressive!

The Play: Declarer wins the ♣K lead with the ♣A and plays the ace of trumps and a trump to the queen. West discards a diamond on the second round of trumps. How would you continue?

East has a trump trick, so you must avoid a heart loser. You play the ♡K and lead a small heart from dummy. If East ruffs in front of your honors, you will be able to draw his last trump and claim the contract. When instead he discards, you win with the ♡A and return to dummy with a diamond. Again you lead a heart towards your remaining heart honor and East cannot beat you by ruffing. When he discards, you win with the ♡Q and ruff your last heart with dummy's ♠8. Whether or not East chooses to overruff, you will lose only one trick (in trumps) and make the slam.

PLAY DEAL 22-4

Neither Vul. Dealer North.

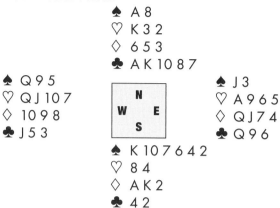

```
                    ♠ A 8
                    ♡ K 3 2
                    ◇ 6 5 3
                    ♣ A K 10 8 7
   ♠ Q 9 5                        ♠ J 3
   ♡ Q J 10 7        N            ♡ A 9 6 5
   ◇ 10 9 8      W       E        ◇ Q J 7 4
   ♣ J 5 3           S            ♣ Q 9 6
                    ♠ K 10 7 6 4 2
                    ♡ 8 4
                    ◇ A K 2
                    ♣ 4 2
```

West	North	East	South
	1♣	pass	1♠
pass	1NT	pass	3♠
pass	4♠	all pass	

The Bidding: When South hears that his partner has a balanced hand of 12-14 points, he judges that his own hand justifies a game try. Should he use 'new minor forcing'? No, because he holds six spades. If partner were to rebid 2NT after 2◇, a continuation of 3♠ would be forcing to game. Instead South invites a game by bidding 3♠ directly. North holds 14 points in prime honor cards and accepts the game try.

The Play: How would you play 4♠ when West leads the ♡Q? There is no real chance that West holds the ♡A, so you do best to play low from dummy on the first two rounds of hearts. Once in a while West will have started with six hearts and the ♡A will fall from East. That does not happen here and you ruff the third round. You are faced with a potential diamond loser and a potential trump loser (you must hope that it is only one). How can you avoid one of these losers?

If clubs break 3-3, you can set up a discard for the losing diamond. You play the ♣A-K and ruff a club in your hand. When the suit breaks 3-3 (hooray!), you continue with the king and ace of trumps. You can then lead an established club to discard your diamond loser. West is welcome to ruff with the master ♠Q. You will lose just two hearts and one trump.

OGUST RESPONSES

We looked at weak two-bids in Chapter 3, mentioning briefly that partner could respond 2NT if he needed the opener to describe his hand further. Here we look at a very popular way in which the opener can do this. Suppose the bidding starts:

Partner	You
2◊, 2♡ or 2♠	2NT
?	

These are the Ogust responses available to partner:

3♣	minimum points, poor suit
3◊	minimum points, good suit
3♡	maximum points, poor suit
3♠	maximum points, good suit
3NT	AKQ of trumps

Just remember that the responder keeps the bidding low when he has a minimum hand. What does 'good suit' mean? To some extent it depends on the vulnerability, also on the standards that you set in the first place. If you insist on 'sound weak two-bids', then a good suit might be AKJ762 instead of KQ8532. If you seek to cause more problems by opening on a wide range of hands, you might regard KQ8532 as a good suit, since you might instead hold Q108654. It is something you must discuss with your partner.

Here is a sample sequence:

Partner	You	
	2♡	♠ 10 9
2NT	3♠	♡ A K J 10 5 4
4♡		◊ J 9 8
		♣ 8 3

You make the Ogust 3♠ response to show maximum points and a good suit. Suppose instead that your hearts were ♡AJ10632, giving you only 6 HCP. You would make the Ogust 3♣ response to show minimum points and a poor suit.

PLAY DEAL 23-1

Both Vul. Dealer South

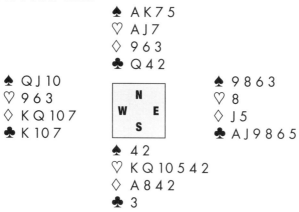

```
                    ♠ A K 7 5
                    ♡ A J 7
                    ◇ 9 6 3
                    ♣ Q 4 2
  ♠ Q J 10                            ♠ 9 8 6 3
  ♡ 9 6 3          N                  ♡ 8
  ◇ K Q 10 7    W     E               ◇ J 5
  ♣ K 10 7          S                 ♣ A J 9 8 6 5
                    ♠ 4 2
                    ♡ K Q 10 5 4 2
                    ◇ A 8 4 2
                    ♣ 3
```

West	North	East	South
			2♡
pass	2NT	pass	3♣
pass	4♡	all pass	

The Bidding: When North hears a vulnerable weak 2♡ opening from his partner, he has a close decision whether to try for game. He decides to take a bold view and bids 2NT to hear more information. Good news arrives when South rebids 3♣, showing a maximum hand with a good suit. North bids 4♡.

The Play: How would you play 4♡ when West leads the ♠Q?

You have three winners in the side suits and six trump tricks. Where can you find a ninth trick? If diamonds break 3-3, the thirteenth diamond will deliver a tenth trick. If diamonds are not 3-3, you can still make ten tricks by ruffing the fourth round of the suit.

You win the spade lead. Should you draw any trumps now? No, because when you subsequently give up two rounds of diamonds, the defenders may be able to play a second and a third round of trumps. You would not then be able to score a diamond ruff in dummy. Instead you should play ace and another diamond.

The defenders cannot defeat the contract. Say that they return a trump. You win and give up another round of diamonds, finding a 4-2 break. West then plays another trump. No problem! You win in your hand and ruff the fourth round of diamonds with dummy's remaining trump honor. You will lose only two diamonds and one club.

PLAY DEAL 23-2

Neither Vul. Dealer South

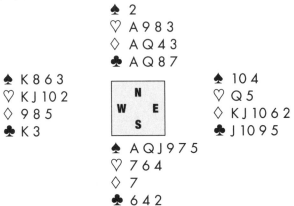

♠ 2
♡ A 9 8 3
♢ A Q 4 3
♣ A Q 8 7

♠ K 8 6 3
♡ K J 10 2
♢ 9 8 5
♣ K 3

♠ 10 4
♡ Q 5
♢ K J 10 6 2
♣ J 10 9 5

♠ A Q J 9 7 5
♡ 7 6 4
♢ 7
♣ 6 4 2

West	North	East	South
			2♠
pass	2NT	pass	3♢
pass	3♠	all pass	

The Bidding: How good is that North hand, facing a non-vulnerable weak 2♠? The first point to note is that it is likely to play poorly in notrump. Even if South's spade suit can be set up for only one loser, there is no reason to expect a side-suit entry to the established cards in the suit. You will do better playing in spades. If partner has a disciplined weak two and five trump tricks can be made, you can add three aces and a possibility of two queen finesses. Partner may even hold a useful card in one of the side suits. North decides to ask for more information and South's 3♢ shows a minimum weak two with a good spade suit. North signs off in 3♠.

The Play: How would you play 3♠ when West leads the ♢9? You win with the ♢A and finesse the ♠Q, losing to the ♠K. West can judge from the 3♢ response that East is likely to hold the ♡Q. (If South held the ♠AQJ and the ♡Q he would have a maximum weak two.) He switches to the ♡2, won with the ♡A. Even though the ♠10 falls, declarer is then in danger of losing one spade, two hearts and two clubs. A winning club finesse comes to the rescue and the contract is just made.

Many players overbid opposite a weak two-bid. This deal is a reminder that you will need a strong hand to make game when you do not have a trump fit.

PLAY DEAL 23-3

E-W Vul. Dealer North

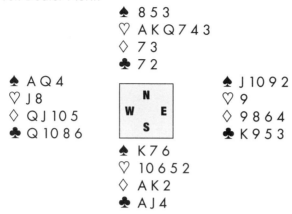

```
                    ♠ 8 5 3
                    ♡ A K Q 7 4 3
                    ◇ 7 3
                    ♣ 7 2
  ♠ A Q 4                              ♠ J 10 9 2
  ♡ J 8              N                 ♡ 9
  ◇ Q J 10 5     W      E              ◇ 9 8 6 4
  ♣ Q 10 8 6        S                  ♣ K 9 5 3
                    ♠ K 7 6
                    ♡ 10 6 5 2
                    ◇ A K 2
                    ♣ A J 4
```

West	North	East	South
	2♡	pass	2NT
pass	3NT	all pass	

The Bidding: Although South holds 15 HCP and four-card heart support, game is by no means guaranteed opposite a weak two-bid. He responds with an Ogust 2NT to discover more about his partner's hand. The unusual 3NT response from North shows the AKQ of trumps. What should South do now? The answer is: Nothing! He should pass 3NT, expecting to score six heart tricks plus the three top winners in his hand.

The Play: Once you reach 3NT, there is nothing much to the play. You win the ◇Q opening lead and claim nine top tricks. (Yes, you might try for an overtrick in some way, but we are not concerned with that here. As the cards lie, only nine tricks can be made.)

See what will happen to any pairs who end in 4♡ instead, playing in the 6-4 trump fit. East will lead the ♠J and the defenders will quickly pocket three tricks in the suit. Declarer has no hope of avoiding a club loser in addition and the heart game goes one down.

'How did you manage to get to 3NT?' you will be asked.

'No problem, was there? We use the Ogust 2NT!'

PLAY DEAL 23-4

N-S Vul. Dealer South

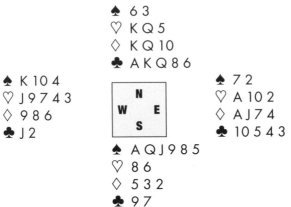

♠ 6 3
♡ K Q 5
◇ K Q 10
♣ A K Q 8 6

♠ K 10 4
♡ J 9 7 4 3
◇ 9 8 6
♣ J 2

♠ 7 2
♡ A 10 2
◇ A J 7 4
♣ 10 5 4 3

♠ A Q J 9 8 5
♡ 8 6
◇ 5 3 2
♣ 9 7

West	North	East	South
			2♠
pass	2NT	pass	3◇
pass	4♠	all pass	

The Bidding: North bids 2NT to ask for further information. South's 3◇ shows a minimum hand (around 6 to a poor 8 HCP) but with good spades. Hoping to lose at most the two red aces and one trump, North jumps to 4♠.

The Play: Look at the defense now from the East seat. Your partner leads the ◇9 and the ◇K is played from dummy. What is your plan to make four defensive tricks and defeat the spade game?

Suppose you win with the ◇A. You cannot continue diamonds effectively from your side of the table. On any return, declarer will be able to draw trumps and eventually discard a diamond loser on dummy's clubs. You know from the Ogust response that South has good trumps. To beat the contract it looks as if you need to score one trump (in partner's hand), along with the ♡A and two diamond tricks in your hand. On this first trick you must refuse to take the ◇A, signaling encouragement with the ◇7.

Declarer cannot take a discard immediately on dummy's clubs because West would ruff. If instead he finesses the ♠Q, your partner will win and play another diamond, allowing you to score two tricks with your ◇AJ. Now you can even cash your ♡A and lead the thirteenth diamond, promoting your partner's ♠10 into another trick for the defense. Down two. Brilliant!

RESPONSIVE DOUBLES

A responsive double is made after partner has overcalled or doubled and RHO has raised the opener's suit. Your double is for takeout.

LHO	Partner	RHO	You
1♠	dbl	2♠	dbl

LHO	Partner	RHO	You
1♠	2♡	2♠	dbl

How strong must you be for a responsive double? It depends on the level of the bidding. If RHO's raise is at the two-level in a minor-suit, you might double on only 6 HCP. When partner will have to rebid at the three-level you would need at least 9 HCP.

A responsive double shows two places to play. In the first auction, partner will expect you to hold both minor suits since if you held hearts, you could bid them. In the second auction above, you would again hold both minor suits (and usually a doubleton heart). It is a matter of partnership agreement how high you will play these responsive doubles. We suggest that you play them up to a level of 3◇.

You		LHO	Partner	RHO	You
♠ Q 9 8 7		1♣	dbl	2♣	dbl
♡ K 10 9 2					
◇ K 3					
♣ 9 4 3					

Your responsive double shows both majors. If partner holds four hearts, say, he will rebid 2♡, 3♡ or 4♡, according to his strength.

You		LHO	Partner	RHO	You
♠ J 9 7 3		1♡	dbl	2♡	2♠
♡ K 10 9					
◇ A 10 8 2					
♣ 8 5					

Here you expect partner to hold spades, so you bid 2♠ rather than doubling.

PLAY DEAL 24-1

N-S Vul. Dealer East

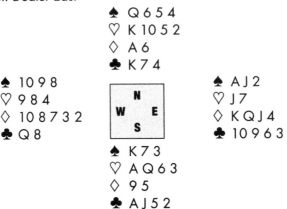

```
              ♠ Q 6 5 4
              ♡ K 10 5 2
              ◇ A 6
              ♣ K 7 4
♠ 10 9 8                      ♠ A J 2
♡ 9 8 4         N            ♡ J 7
◇ 10 8 7 3 2  W   E          ◇ K Q J 4
♣ Q 8           S            ♣ 10 9 6 3
              ♠ K 7 3
              ♡ A Q 6 3
              ◇ 9 5
              ♣ A J 5 2
```

West	North	East	South
		1◇	dbl
3◇	dbl	pass	3♡
pass	4♡	all pass	

The Bidding: South makes a takeout double of 1◇ and West raises preemptively to 3◇. North does not want to choose which major to make trumps and contests the auction with a responsive double (a form of takeout double). South has a fairly minimum double and bids just 3♡, which is non-forcing. North is then happy to raise to game in hearts.

The Play: West leads the ♠10 and declarer plays low from dummy. East does not want to play his ♠A because this would allow declarer to score tricks with both the ♠Q and the ♠K. He therefore follows with the ♠2, South winning with the ♠K. How would you continue the play, as declarer?

You draw trumps in three rounds and turn to the club suit. Your intention is to score three club tricks, which will allow you to discard dummy's diamond loser. Suppose you cross to the ♣K and finesse the ♣J. You will make the three club tricks that you need if the finesse wins, and also when the finesse loses but clubs break 3-3.

You can do better than this by starting with the ace and king of clubs. This gives you the additional chance of making the contract when West began with a doubleton ♣Q. (If the ♣Q does not drop, you will lead towards the ♣J on the third round.)

PLAY DEAL 24-2

E-W Vul. Dealer West

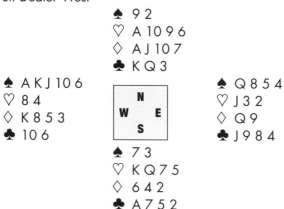

	♠ 9 2	
	♡ A 10 9 6	
	◇ A J 10 7	
	♣ K Q 3	

♠ A K J 10 6
♡ 8 4
◇ K 8 5 3
♣ 10 6

♠ Q 8 5 4
♡ J 3 2
◇ Q 9
♣ J 9 8 4

♠ 7 3
♡ K Q 7 5
◇ 6 4 2
♣ A 7 5 2

West	North	East	South
1♠	dbl	2♠	3♡
pass	4♡	all pass	

The Bidding: West holds a good spade suit and a four-card side suit headed by an honor. He is therefore happy to open 1♠ despite holding only 11 HCP. North doubles and East raises to 2♠. Should you make a responsive double on the South cards? No, because you expect partner to hold hearts and you have four hearts too. If you did double, partner would probably bid 3◇, not reading you for four hearts. North raises you to game in hearts, ending the auction.

The Play: West scores his two top spades and then switches to the ♣10. How will you play?

You win with dummy's ♣K and draw trumps in three rounds, ending in the South hand. You will be able to ruff the fourth round of clubs, if necessary, so all depends on your handling of the diamond suit. You lead a diamond to the jack and East wins with the queen. When he returns the ♣J you win in your hand and take a second diamond finesse, leading to the ◇10. This time the finesse wins. You will make the game with four trump tricks, two diamonds, three clubs and a club ruff in dummy.

PLAY DEAL 24-3

Both Vul. Dealer North

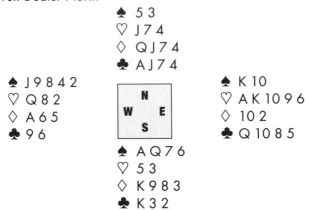

```
                    ♠ 5 3
                    ♡ J 7 4
                    ◇ Q J 7 4
                    ♣ A J 7 4
♠ J 9 8 4 2                              ♠ K 10
♡ Q 8 2              N                   ♡ A K 10 9 6
◇ A 6 5          W     E                 ◇ 10 2
♣ 9 6               S                    ♣ Q 10 8 5
                    ♠ A Q 7 6
                    ♡ 5 3
                    ◇ K 9 8 3
                    ♣ K 3 2
```

West	North	East	South
	pass	1♡	dbl
2♡	dbl	pass	3◇
all pass			

The Bidding: West raises the hearts, knowing there is at least a 5-3 fit there. North has enough to contest the auction but he does not want to guess which minor suit to bid. He makes a responsive double. South realizes that North would have bid spades (the 'other major') if he held four cards in that suit, expecting South to hold four spades for his original takeout double. Asked to choose a minor suit, South bids 3◇.

The Play: How would you play 3◇ when West leads the ♣9?

The club finesse is obviously wrong. You win with dummy's ♣A and finesse the ♠Q successfully. When you play the ♠A, the ♠K falls from East. It seems that East may have started with a doubleton spade. You lead the ♠6 and ruff with dummy's ◇J to avoid a cheap overruff. East does indeed show out, pitching a heart. Since you intend to ruff another spade with dummy's ◇Q, your next move is to lead a low trump from dummy and finesse the ◇9. West wins with the ◇A and plays his remaining club. You win with the ♣K and ruff your last spade with dummy's ◇Q. You then draw the remaining trumps and make the contract, losing just two hearts, one trump and a club.

PLAY DEAL 24-4

E-W Vul. Dealer East

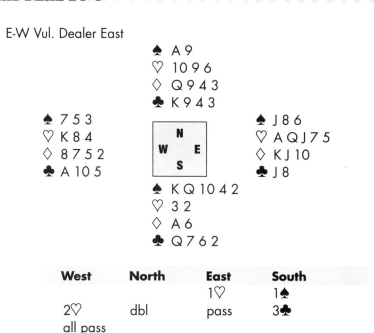

```
                    ♠ A 9
                    ♡ 10 9 6
                    ◇ Q 9 4 3
                    ♣ K 9 4 3
♠ 7 5 3                             ♠ J 8 6
♡ K 8 4          N                  ♡ A Q J 7 5
◇ 8 7 5 2     W     E               ◇ K J 10
♣ A 10 5         S                  ♣ J 8
                    ♠ K Q 10 4 2
                    ♡ 3 2
                    ◇ A 6
                    ♣ Q 7 6 2
```

West	North	East	South
		1♡	1♠
2♡	dbl	pass	3♣
all pass			

The Bidding: North would not be happy allowing East-West to play in 2♡. Indeed, the contract would have been made easily, with declarer scoring five hearts, two diamonds and the ♣A. North contests with a responsive double (also sometimes called a 'competitive double' when made opposite an overcall by partner). Expecting North to hold both the minor suits, South rebids 3♣ and this ends the auction.

The Play: The defenders have a chance to beat this contract. Take the East cards and see if you would have found the winning defense. Your partner leads the ♡4 and you win with the ♡A. What next?

Declarer may well hold the ◇A. There is a danger that he will be able to discard three diamonds from dummy on his spade suit. You would like to set up a defensive trick in diamonds but the first lead in this suit probably needs to be made by West. You should therefore return the ♡7 to West's ♡K at Trick 2. Knowing that no further heart tricks can be taken, he should then switch to the ◇8. This will establish a diamond trick for you. After this smart defense declarer cannot avoid the loss of two hearts, one diamond and two clubs. He will be one down. This is still a better result for North-South than allowing you to make 2♡.

LEAD-DIRECTING DOUBLES

When your opponents voluntarily bid a slam it is seldom very profitable to double for penalties. You will be happy enough to defeat the contract. Most players therefore use a double of a slam as a *lead-directing double* (known as a Lightner Double). Such a double asks for an *unusual* lead. It specifically tells partner: 'Do not lead any suit that we have bid and do not lead a trump.'

When partner makes a Lightner Double, what suit should you lead? Often he will want you to lead the first suit bid by dummy. If dummy has not bid a suit but declarer has bid a side suit, he is asking for that lead. If no side suits have been bid, your partner will usually be void in one of those suits. You must judge from your own suit lengths where partner's void is likely to be.

LHO	Partner	RHO	You
1♡	pass	1♠	pass
3♠	pass	4NT	pass
5♣	pass	6♠	pass
pass	dbl		

Partner's double asks for a lead in hearts, dummy's first-bid suit.

Suppose instead that your RHO had carried the bidding to 6NT. A double would still ask for a heart lead. You would double with ♡AK or perhaps with ♡AQ, hoping that the ♡K would be in the dummy.

The same principle applies when the opponents bid freely to 3NT. A double by the defender not on lead will ask for a particular lead:
- If the doubler has bid, he asks you to lead his suit.
- If you have bid, he asks you to lead your suit.
- If neither of you has bid, you should lead dummy's first bid suit.
- If the bidding is a simple 1NT – 3NT, partner has a great suit somewhere and is asking you to lead your shortest suit, hoping to find his strength.

Whenever the opponents make an artificial bid (Stayman, a transfer, a fourth-suit forcing bid, a control-showing cuebid or a Blackwood response), you will have the opportunity to double to show strength in that suit. If you had a chance to double a Blackwood 5♡ response and did not double, partner might decide against a heart for his opening lead.

PLAY DEAL 25-1

E-W Vul. Dealer North

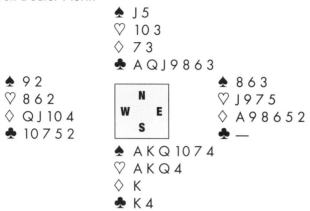

♠ J 5
♡ 10 3
◇ 7 3
♣ A Q J 9 8 6 3

♠ 9 2
♡ 8 6 2
◇ Q J 10 4
♣ 10 7 5 2

♠ 8 6 3
♡ J 9 7 5
◇ A 9 8 6 5 2
♣ —

♠ A K Q 10 7 4
♡ A K Q 4
◇ K
♣ K 4

West	North	East	South
	3♣	pass	3♠
pass	4♠	pass	4NT
pass	5♣	pass	6♠
pass	pass	dbl	all pass

The Bidding: South's 3♠ is forcing. Expecting a six-card suit opposite, North raises the spades. South uses RKCB to ask for keycards and hears of one ace (1430 responses are being used). He is then happy to bid 6♠.

The auction is not yet over! East sees a splendid chance of beating the slam if he can persuade partner to lead a club. He makes a lead-directing double (known here as a Lightner Double). Without such a double, West would doubt-less have led the ◇Q. He will now lead dummy's suit, clubs, fully expecting his partner to ruff.

The Play: West leads the ♣2 and East ruffs. He promptly cashes the ◇A and the slam goes one down. Lightner strikes again!

PLAY DEAL 25-2

E-W Vul. Dealer North

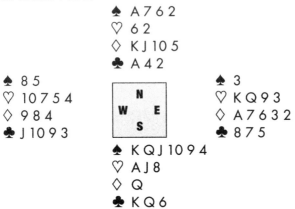

```
              ♠ A 7 6 2
              ♡ 6 2
              ♢ K J 10 5
              ♣ A 4 2
♠ 8 5                          ♠ 3
♡ 10 7 5 4        N           ♡ K Q 9 3
♢ 9 8 4      W        E       ♢ A 7 6 3 2
♣ J 10 9 3        S           ♣ 8 7 5
              ♠ K Q J 10 9 4
              ♡ A J 8
              ♢ Q
              ♣ K Q 6
```

West	North	East	South
	1♢	pass	1♠
pass	2♠	pass	4NT
pass	5♡	dbl	6♠
all pass			

The Bidding: South is delighted to hear his partner raise the spades. He decides to bid a slam provided two aces are not missing. Partner's 5♡ shows two aces and East (wide awake for such a chance) doubles this artificial response to suggest a heart lead. South advances to 6♠, nevertheless.

The Play: Without East's lead-directing double, West might well have led the ♣J. As it is, he leads the ♡4 to East's ♡Q and South's ♡A. Declarer draws trumps with the ace and king and, without much hope, leads the ♢5 from dummy. A few milliseconds later, East has scored the ♢A and the ♡K. The slam is one down.

East would have made the same double of 5♡ even if he did not hold the ♢A. Move the ♢A to the West hand and, of course, it still requires a heart lead to beat the slam.

PLAY DEAL 25-3

E-W Vul. Dealer South

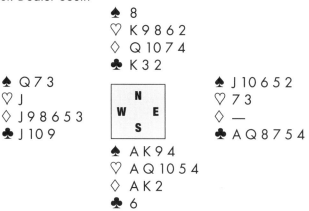

```
                    ♠ 8
                    ♡ K 9 8 6 2
                    ◇ Q 10 7 4
                    ♣ K 3 2
  ♠ Q 7 3                        ♠ J 10 6 5 2
  ♡ J              N             ♡ 7 3
  ◇ J 9 8 6 5 3  W   E           ◇ —
  ♣ J 10 9         S             ♣ A Q 8 7 5 4
                    ♠ A K 9 4
                    ♡ A Q 10 5 4
                    ◇ A K 2
                    ♣ 6
```

West	North	East	South
			1♡
pass	4♡	pass	4NT
pass	5♣	pass	6♡
pass	pass	dbl	all pass

The Bidding: South holds a great hand but with a potential loser in every suit he is not quite strong enough to bid 2♣. He opens 1♡ and North shows a fairly weak hand with five-card trump support when he leaps to 4♡. South asks for keycards and ends the auction with a bid of 6♡. Wait a moment, the bidding is not yet over! East has a void diamond and expects the slam to go down if West can find a diamond lead. He makes a Lightner Double, suggesting that he holds a side-suit void somewhere.

The Play: Take the West cards now. Look just at your own thirteen cards and decide what you would have led after partner's double of 6♡. Why has he doubled? A double of a freely bid slam is Lightner. It asks you to find an unusual lead, often in a suit that your partner can ruff.

Here you have six diamonds and only three cards in the other two side suits. It's not a close decision. You lead a diamond and you are pleased to see that partner ruffs. Your enjoyment increases as partner cashes the ♣A at Trick 2 and the slam goes one down. This was no time for East to be greedy, returning a major suit in the hope that he could enjoy two club tricks later! Declarer would have drawn trumps and discarded his singleton club on the fourth round of diamonds.

PLAY DEAL 25-4

N-S Vul. Dealer South

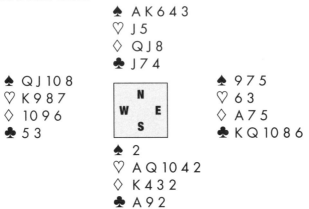

♠ A K 6 4 3
♡ J 5
◊ Q J 8
♣ J 7 4

♠ Q J 10 8
♡ K 9 8 7
◊ 10 9 6
♣ 5 3

♠ 9 7 5
♡ 6 3
◊ A 7 5
♣ K Q 10 8 6

♠ 2
♡ A Q 10 4 2
◊ K 4 3 2
♣ A 9 2

West	North	East	South
			1♡
pass	1♠	pass	2◊
pass	3♣	dbl	3NT
all pass			

The Bidding: North bids a fourth-suit-forcing 3♣ to investigate the best game. Is East asleep? No! He doubles 3♣ to request a club lead against the eventual contract. South bids 3NT, ending the auction.

The Play: West leads the ♣5, East playing the ♣10. Declarer holds up the ♣A for a couple of rounds, hoping that West holds the ◊A. It does him no good on this lie of the cards and the contact goes two down.

Suppose that North-South had found their way to 4♡ instead, warned by East's lead-directing double. A club lead is the only one to sink that contract too! Perhaps declarer will win the second club and play dummy's ♠AK, throwing his last club. When the ♡J is run to the ♡K, West will force declarer with a spade. Down to the same trump length as West, and with no diamond tricks yet scored, he will lose control and go one down.

Remember the concepts you learned in this book with the handy...

Pocket Guide to Bridge Conventions You Should Know

978-1-897106-65-5
Barbara Seagram & Marc Smith
USD 9.95 CAD 9.95 GBP 6.95

Also available:

Pocket Guide to Even More Conventions

978-1-77140-023-7
Barbara Seagram & David Bird
USD 9.95 CAD 9.95 GBP 6.95

Pocket Guide to Declarer Play

978-1-77140-002-2
Barbara Seagram & David Bird
USD 9.95 CAD 9.95 GBP 6.95

Pocket Guide to Defensive Play

978-1-77140-004-6
Barbara Seagram & David Bird
USD 9.95 CAD 9.95 GBP 6.95

Get More Practice with Quizbooks from Master Point Press

Bidding at Bridge: A Quizbook

978-1-77140-018-3
Barbara Seagram & David Bird
USD 15.95 CAD 15.95 GBP 9.95

This book gives the near-beginner a chance to practice principles on which sound bidding is based, from the opening bid onward.

Declarer Play at Bridge: A Quizbook

978-1-897106-91-4
Barbara Seagram & David Bird
USD 15.95 CAD 15.95 GBP 9.95

A quizbook to accompany the award-winning *Planning the Play of a Bridge Hand*, by the same author team. Named the 2013 American Bridge Teachers' Association Book of the Year. Readers practice principles of sound declarer play: count your winners, count your losers, make a plan.

Defensive Play at Bridge: A Quizbook

978-1-897106-92-1
Barbara Seagram & David Bird
USD 15.95 CAD 15.95 GBP 9.95

Covers the basics of defense, defending against notrump contracts and defending against suit contracts. Each section contains a brief introduction of its topic, and ideas are reinforced with quiz hands accompanied by carefully explained solutions and helpful tips throughout.

The 25 Series from Master Point Press

 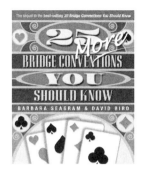 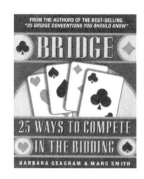

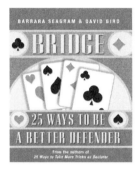 

By Barbara Seagram & Marc Smith:

25 Conventions You Should Know
978-1-894154-07-9 USD 19.95 CAD 21.95 GBP 11.95

25 Ways to Compete in the Bidding
978-1-894154-22-2 USD 19.95 CAD 21.95 GBP 11.95

By Barbara Seagram & David Bird:

25 MORE Conventions You Should Know
978-1-894154-65-9 USD 19.95 CAD 21.95 GBP 11.95

25 Ways to Be a Better Defender
978-1-897106-11-2 USD 19.95 CAD 21.95 GBP 11.95

25 Ways to Take More Tricks as Declarer
978-1-894154-47-5 USD 19.95 CAD 21.95 GBP 11.95

CONTACT US

Master Point Press
214 Merton St. Suite 205
Toronto, ON M4S 1A6
(647) 956-4933

Master Point Press on the Internet

www.masterpointpress.com

Our main site, with information about our books and software, reviews and more.

www.teachbridge.com

Our site for bridge teachers and students — free downloadable support material for our books, helpful articles and more.

www.bridgeblogging.com

Read and comment on regular articles from MPP authors and other bridge notables.

www.ebooksbridge.com

Purchase downloadable electronic versions of MPP books and software.